A MYSTICAL TALE OF FINDING ONE TRUE LOVE IN...

DIVINE TIME

DIVINE TIME

This is a work of fiction. Characters, institutions and organisations, including names, places and events mentioned in this novel are either products of the author's imagination used fictitiously without any intent to describe actual individuals or conduct. Any resemblance to actual persons, living or dead, events, or locales is entirely coincidental.

First paperback edition published September 2021

NomadSoulWarrior, Author

Edited by Jon Di Luca

Cover illustration by Alina Drozdova

Cover design and formatting: Stone Ridge Books LLC

ISBN: 9798532969308

A MYSTICAL TALE OF FINDING ONE TRUE LOVE IN...

DIVINE TIME

NOMADSOULWARRIOR

Take a deep breath...
Now, ready yourself to discover the mystic within
As each line in this book unfolds
Allow your imagination to soar along
and co-create a... limitless destiny

-NomadSoulWarrior

O

She sat by a crackling fire, humming softly, basking in the Moon's bright cosmic waves. Lushly illuminated stone monuments surrounded her, penetrating the night sky

She blinked, gradually surrendering, letting her eyelids close. Her thoughts trailed off into spiraling vibrant sparks of astral light towards the unknown

Leisurely, she rose to her feet, swaying to inner celestial music. Sublime energy pulsed through her head - torso - thighs - down to the tip of her fingers. Feeling limitless and unbound by physical barriers, she drifted off towards a beautiful golden light… A bright powerful flowering oblivion took hold of her being

Ultimately, the feeling of being utterly captured and consumed by a force larger than herself proved to be disorienting. She wavered. Her longing to seize the moment was disrupted as she tried to regain balance. A momentary dull uncertainty hit her...

Not Yet, I'm not ready...

The next morning's warm breeze caressed her body. She stretched as she opened her eyes slowly, languidly running her fingers up from the smooth skin of her bare belly to her modestly covered breasts

Once she felt fully present and aware of her surroundings, she reached out to a rock nearby for support. Without hurry, she rose to her feet and headed for home

She reached into her cinch pouch, pulling out a gold coin stamped with a dragon emblem. Whenever she felt anxious or uncertain, holding this coin calmed her down, gave her the sense that all is well, and reminded her to trust herself. It was a gift from her uncle, the governor of Orbalunei...She treasured it

As she approached her village, she knew she needed to come back to reality. She spotted some wild herbs, picking some as she went. Orbalunei was the name of her village, a composition of wondrously carved cave dwelling at the foot of a mountain

By one particularly craggy bend of the road home, she noticed some mules being led along the roadside carrying heavy loads of hemp fabric on their backs. The dusty vision of the nomadic merchants brought memories of her earlier life... *mother leaving...* She pushed them back into the past where they had been, and instead, tried to let herself savor the bright colors of the cloths and the musky scents of the small caravan

Whilst stopping by the well at the village centre to get a drink of cool water, she heard a cheerful, musical voice calling her name

"Ariara! Where are you coming from so early in the morning?"

It was her neighbor, Mandana. Full of joy, as usual

"Oh... I fell asleep out in the valley. The moon was so beautiful last night. I had to go out there and get a closer look"

Though she was unsure of what Mandana would think of her fabulous experience, she couldn't help telling her. She continued as if entranced, "Lately I've been having these little bonfire dance rituals during the full moon, but... this time was different. I saw a beautiful, magnificent golden light. I walked towards it but I lost my balance and... well, next thing I knew it was morning"

Mandana's eyes grew wide. "Like Dunya..." She said, half to herself

"Who?"

"The woman who used to live in your cave. She left a few years before you came to the village. Haven't you seen her sketchings on the wall?"

"Sketchings?"

"Behind the tapestry"

"Behind the tapestry? Please, Mandana, show me... tell me..."

They entered Ariara's cave together. By the entry was an enormous window, providing a sweeping view of Love Valley. Near that window was a beautiful tapestry

"I wove this... as a gift to Dunya," Mandana stated proudly with a hint of nostalgia

"I love this, Mandana. I didn't know you made it"

"Thank you. I used to weave a lot... Haven't done much lately"

Ariara gasped when Mandana moved one side to unveil Dunya's sketchings: blazing light from the moon cascading over the valley. She was instantly reminded of the night before

"That's the golden light that I saw! Please Mandana, tell me more about her. Dunya..."

"Oh, That's quite a story. Dunya..." Mandana searched for the right words, "Dunya appeared in the village as an orphan. She was taken in by Mariano and Marrietta, the elderly couple who used to live here in this cave. We became dear friends... I really miss her... After Mariano and Marietta passed on, Dunya lived on her own. She spent a lot of time alone in the valley... she'd come home and tell these fantastic stories of visionary dreams that she would have..."

"Visionary dreams?"

"Visions? Dreams? Voyages? We were never sure what to

call them. I loved to hear about them. Your uncle too... became fascinated by her story. He became a frequent visitor..."

Ariara traced the sketching, enamored, "What happened to her? Please, tell me more... Tell me about her visions"

"Hmm well, she talked about another world, people she met, their peculiar ways of living. Dunya loved fabrics and materials, so she would always give detailed descriptions of their clothing. I was more interested in hearing about their complex dwellings, oh and then there was the water..." Mandana laughed

"The water?"

"She said people carried it around in something called 'bottles'. They were like invisible jars"

"Bottles? That's a funny word"

"Then there were *machines* and *devices*. I forgot which one did what, but some could communicate through vast distances... and some moved from place to place on big wheels. I think those were 'machines', and 'devices' were the ones they talked to each other on... I'm sorry, I can't remember exactly... Oh, I miss her..."

Ariara was surprised to see Mandana suddenly at the verge of tears. She rushed over to comfort her. Mandana smiled and gathered her thoughts

"There's one thing I'll always remember her saying, though I never quite understood it, and it had nothing to do with this fabulous other world…"

"What was that?"

"'Be free. Let tomorrow take care of itself.' Then suddenly, 7 years ago, she vanished. Free-spirited person that she was, God knows where she's gone off to"

"Nobody looked for her?"

"She mostly kept to herself. Only your uncle and I noticed she was gone. Oh… and Aries, the Shepherd's boy. He said that he saw her on the day she vanished. He told us some wild story, but he was young. You know, he might have been just trying to get the grown ups' attention"

"Oh, that cute little boy. He is always asking me about my herb garden. What did he say? His wild story…"

"That's enough stories for today Ariara, maybe next time.

I have to run. I want to see what's new in the market - heard some traders have arrived. Oh, I almost forgot why I came to visit today… I have a slight tummy ache…"

Ariara smiled, though she was disappointed at Mandana's sudden reluctance. She wrapped up some fresh mint leaves for her

"Alrighty Mandana, But I want to hear more next time! Glad you stopped by! Stay safe"

Ariara couldn't help being fascinated by Mandana's story about Dunya and the mysterious etchings behind the tapestry

They must be related to the golden light somehow…

She tried to occupy her mind with her usual gardening routine - picking flowers and herbs, then drying, infusing, and organizing them according to their healing properties

Her elemental connection with herbs had already made her a respected healer, despite only living there for a few years. The villagers looked to her for relief from all kinds of ailments, bruises and pains. Her instinctive desire to listen and extend her energy to those in need was highly regarded. Also, like Mandana, sometimes they would come to her just to talk about life - trusting her wisdom, though she was young

But now, she couldn't stop herself from ruminating about Dunya and her 'otherworldly visions'. *What was in the Love Valley that gave Dunya such visions... what could she have seen in the other world out there?*

She discreetly searched for Aries, the shepherd's boy. Maybe he would have some clues to Dunya's disappearance. *After all, nobody else would know about the Golden Light, they wouldn't know...* Sadly, she discovered that he was away with his family to bring some of their sheep to be shorn, and he wouldn't be back for a few weeks

Those weeks passed. Some of her herbal infusions were ready. She spent one whole day straining oils into jars. She found great pleasure in this, softly chanting as she closed each one tight. It was dark when she was done. She sat by the window to rest and gaze

Moonbeams shone through the panorama of the Love Valley. She took a brief look at the sketches on the wall, back up to the sky and knew she had to get going

She walked to her usual spot, started a bonfire, sat on a familiar rock, straightened her back, laid her hands on her thighs, and surrendered to the stillness of the night. As she swept her hair up with her left hand, a gentle night breeze caressed her neck and bare shoulders

She took a deep breath, got to her feet and gradually disrobed as she danced and whirled. Swaying now, her gaze turned towards the moon. She felt herself drifting off towards that same beautiful golden light. This time, without looking back, she whirled into oblivion

Part I

Ariara opened her eyes and jumped up to her feet. Immediately, she realized she was not in Love Valley. A vast grassland stretched before her, as far as she could see

A sumptuous breeze helped her transition from feeling slightly anxious, not knowing where she was or how she got there, to allowing the awe of this new exotic scenery to fill her with confidence and enthusiasm. She was immediately delighted by the fresh scent of the dewy air, savoring the taste of the purest conscious breaths she had ever taken

The rustling sounds of the grass charged the surrounding. She fixed her hair away from her face and looked back behind her to see... *Is this a rock? This is so massive, its shadow would cover all of Orbalunei*

It wasn't merely a rock. It was gigantic, monumental, bigger than anything she'd ever seen before, an endless wall up to the sky. She tried to find her way behind it - but it was too big to get around

Encouraged by the warmth of the sun, she ventured away from the Grand Stone towards the open fields. Alone in a vast space, she began walking towards the open fields without any specific direction...

After some time of wandering blissfully lost, she began to feel thirsty. She assessed her belongings, searching for something to drink. All she found was her cinch pouch wrapped around her right wrist

Suddenly, a woman appeared from nowhere. She wore a headdress of pale feathers and a white dress that put her in complete harmony with the brilliant sun shining behind her

The woman spoke in a melodious and carefree tone, "Wow, what a pretty tunic! Is that hemp?"

Ariara, though slightly surprised by the abrupt appearance, felt immediately comfortable in the presence of this new stranger. She welcomed the compliment, and didn't hesitate to engage in pleasant conversation. After all, she was quite fond of her tunic

"Hi, yes, thank you. My mother made this for me, years ago..."

Suddenly she remembered where she was - or rather - where she wasn't... "I'm sorry, I seem to be lost. I woke up by that Grand Stone. Just a little while ago. I'm very thirsty. Would you know of any nearby wells?"

"Here... I have a bottle, have some of mine..." The woman handed her a bottle

Ariara's mind was aflutter as she drank with vigor in a state of disbelief... *A bottle? Is this the world that Mandana was talking about? I must be having a dream...*

She was astonished at the plastic receptacle, squeezed it before handing it back, "Thank you. I'm Ariara"

"Such a lovely name...Pleased to meet you Ariara. I'm Agnes"

Ariara gave a pleased, shy, and slightly puzzled smile. "Agnes... I've never heard that name. I like it"

"It's supposed to mean pure, like an angel. The very first person I met here gave me that name"

"Who? What do you mean, gave you that name?"

"Let's just say, I was once wandering, lost and thirsty, as you are now and I met a friendly stranger. When he asked me my name I was tongue tied. He told me I look like an Agnes, and I smiled, so the name stuck with me"

Ariara felt invigorated by this fresh encounter and the cool water, "How do you know which direction to go? Everything here looks the same… all flat lands filled with grass?"

"Don't you see the Mount up ahead?" Agnes smiled coyly. Her silver strands beautifully caught the sunlight, her dark hair flowing down her shoulders

"The Mount?" Ariara was shocked to see, up ahead in the distance, a giant blurry visage. "How did I miss that?"

"What's important is that you see it now. The person I told you about, the one who calls me Agnes, is there waiting for me, along with another friend. Would you like to join us for lunch?"

"Yes please, that's so kind of you. Thank you"

They walked for a bit. Agnes didn't say much. There was so much that Ariara wanted to ask, but she was too awestruck by the scenery. The sun and the breeze felt so good, the grass smelled so fresh

As they drew closer to the Mount, a man, waving his arms in greeting, approached them

"Where did you wander off to, Agnes? Jiemba said you went for a quick walk. I'm starving" the man laughed as he gave Agnes a light hug

This must be the man who gave her her name...

Agnes whispered "No that's not him"

It was as if she had heard her inner thoughts. Ariara was stunned. *Did I say that out loud?*

Agnes turned back to her handsome friend, "Well I suppose it wasn't so quick, and a good thing too... I found a new friend"

Ariara looked at the man, bashfully curious, as he lightly raked and tousled his own dark brown hair. The expression on his face naturally radiated forth a happy spirit. His eyes, intense and gentle, met her gaze. She was struck by a soothing softness inside

"Well, hello new friend, I'm Etoile," he said with a charming, thick, and gentle voice

"I'm Ariara"

She bent her head lightly to hide her blush as he held her gaze and extended a strong hand that she gladly received in hers. She felt like she was melting

Agnes led with a wave of her hand and they walked on. Etoile strode beside warmly, gushing over Ariara

The three arrived at the Mount

Ariara stopped still for a moment to admire what stood before her. In the middle of what felt like absolutely nowhere stood an enormous cluster of ochre-colored mounds

A mild summer breeze ushered them through one of the dry creek beds towards the centre. The giant mounds concealed a vast open space where sleeping tents lined the shadows. Tables and chairs scattered near food stalls whilst people tended to fruit, food and a myriad of other fragrant delights

Ariara felt a sudden surge of excitement flowing through her veins. Enthralled, she was drawn to join the crowd. She looked back and saw Etoile standing close

He placed his hand gently on her shoulder and lifted his chiseled jaw into a smile, "Do you like what you see?"

Every single bit

High noon. People were gathering for lunch, queueing up at the stalls buying freshly made food. Delicious scents wafted through the air. Agnes returned to their table, smiling, arms loaded

"I got us a little bit of everything. Kangaroo pies, Croc Dogs, Cranberry salad...Let's dive in"

Ariara eyed the exotic food eagerly. Though the dishes were unfamiliar, it all smelled quite good. She took her seat next to Agnes

"Hey hey hey"

A new jovial voice popped in. It belonged to a tall, well-built man in a pale blue shirt and khaki shorts. He hugged Agnes and kissed her on the forehead. She wrapped her arm lightly around his waist, rested her head lovingly on his shoulder and made introductions

"This is Ariara. I met her on my little jaunt this morning." Agnes arched her eyebrows towards the man to answer Ariara's inner question, as if to say, 'Yes dear, this is the man I was talking about'

"Glad to meet you, Ariara. I'm Jiemba," he greeted her warmly, flashed a caring smile and quickly snapped a photo of her

"What was that?" *Is that a machine or a device?*

"Oh, just to capture that smile…" he winked at her, and let his camera hang back around his neck

A sense of familiarity filled her as she looked into Jiemba's eyes. *Same twinkle as Uncle. He must be the one she mentioned, the one who gave her the name Agnes*

Jiemba took the seat across Agnes - surveyed the food. "Ah! My Angel!!" he winked at Agnes and brushed her chin with his fingers. "You always get my favorite." Her eyes radiated joy in return

Soon, Etoile joined them as well, "Long queue! But it's worth it. There's nothing like lemon squash in this hot weather!" He heartily placed the cold drinks on the table, opened one can and handed it to Ariara. She thanked him amiably

Agnes filled Ariara's plate, "Try them all and see which one you like best"

Ariara smiled appreciatively as she slipped a small portion of pie on her fork. She snuck a glance at Etoile, and caught him staring at her, pleased with his view. He quickly looked down to his plate and picked up a slice of pie. A sly smile spread across his lips

After the sumptuous meal, they strolled around the area. Ariara was moved to a quaint ecstasy by the diversity of colors

in the people's clothing. She let herself get lost in the relaxing mood of the idyllic summer afternoon. There were small groups chatting, whilst others took naps in makeshift huts

As they walked, Ariara noticed some uniquely shaped stones along the way. She picked up a few. Agnes observed her delight as she opened her pouch to place them in

"Collecting lovely treasures, I see"

"I love collecting little things I find along my path. This way, whenever I open up this pouch, I can relive the good feelings I had when I found them. I suppose I get to enjoy them the second time around"

She showed some of her stones and coins to Agnes

Agnes eyed the Dragon coin. She put her arm around Ariara's shoulder and spoke in a hushed tone

"That coin is rare"

"It was a birthday present from my uncle" Ariara was surprised at how Agnes knew about the coin. "Have you seen one of these before?"

"The story goes… In a land far from here, a mystic was known to live in the mountains. The king bade his men to seek out this mystic for her prediction. They came back with a note sealed with the mystic's blood marked with a Dragon holding its heart. These gold coins were specially stamped with this symbol to attest reverence for the oracle's prediction"

"What was her prediction?"

"Your deepest doubts proved. Love whom You Trust. Uphold Your Truth"

"Deepest doubts?"

"The ruler had dreamt about his wife sneaking around with his most trusted guard, but kept his suspicion to himself. The day he received the mystic's note, he caught them in the act. The Dragon coin was made in honor of the mystic's insight, to mark the day that truth prevailed"

"My uncle told me it represents Truth… And, I've heard a similar story back in my village…"

Agnes seemed to look off into a distant nostalgic reverie briefly, but she soon turned back to Ariara and smiled. "It's great that you keep these tokens of memories, but remember to be free. Tomorrow will take care of itself"

That sounds familiar too… Where have I heard that?

Agnes leaned closer towards her and whispered, "Now, pack up those little trinkets of yours." She gestured towards Etoile who was obviously, yet subtly, trying to get Ariara's attention. "Looks like someone is eager to have more of your time. You don't wanna miss out on that one"

She gave her a teasing smile and winked at her before moving over to casually stroll beside Jiemba

Night fell. A large crowd gathered, illuminated by bonfires

Barefoot musicians in full body paint and loincloths began to play haunting music from long hollow wind instruments

Jiemba was unabashedly exuberant as he found a cozy spot on the ground and invited Agnes to sit down next to him. She lovingly obliged, whispering, loud enough for Ariara to hear, "This is my favorite place to be... Wandering. Drawn to..."

A place you've never wandered

Etoile was beaming. He snuggled in close to Ariara and spoke softly, "Don't be scared, we are just getting back to basics, escaping modern life for a bit"

She smiled bashfully, not quite understanding what he meant, but thrilled to be sitting next to him

"The ritual is bringing me some fortune. I think you are starting to like me," he teased

"That's what I'm more scared of!" She laughed at his boldness, fully embracing the way he made her smile. The music connected her to the earth, to the ground. She felt at peace

Suddenly, the men in body paint and loincloths gathered near the centre fire, chanting and raising smoky cauldrons

"Aha, now you are scared. Don't worry, they are doing that to protect our space and chase away evil spirits"

"I told you I'm not scared..." She squeezed his hand tightly

The crowd's excitement grew as the men engaged in a mock battle with wooden sticks

"They are not really going to kill each other... it's just a show..."

"That's good to know"

The night deepened. Whilst the performers rested, the crowd rose to dance barefoot around the fires. Jiemba and Agnes were among the first and freest

Ariara, under the sacred spell of the space, continued to sit on, relaxing, enjoying the music. Etoile on the other hand, was inspired to move with her

"Well, now that the evil spirits are gone, would you care to dance with me?"

"Only if you teach me how"

"You're in good hands, my dear"

This man knows what to say to make me melt inside

She extended her hand to him and they rose and walked

towards the crowd. Still holding her hand, he pulled her towards him, wrapped his arms around her and steered both their bodies into synchronicity. She put her head on his chest, they danced for a while... a while longer

Once the crowd started to settle back, they rejoined Jiemba and Agnes

A slight chill cooled the night air. Etoile placed a scarf on her back, sat close, holding her hand. The tone of the music changed, deepened, soft and thunderous, as if the earth was speaking from its core, calling all the heavenly elements to join its song

Ariara was spellbound... *This is exactly where I want to be at this very moment*

Morning? Am I still dreaming?

Ariara stepped out of a tent, into a bustling crowd of people packing up their tents, picking up rubbish, loading up their luggage into... *What were these large carts?* She tried to remember what Mandana had shared about Dunya's story. *These must be 'machines'.. They look sturdy. I guess they use these instead of...*

"They call them cars," Agnes said, appearing beside her. "There's an engine that keeps them going, definitely a lot faster than donkeys and mules"

She did it again!! Can Agnes read my mind? Ariara gasped. Before she could ask any further questions, Agnes handed her a bag. "I got you some fruits... I reckoned you'd be hungry when you woke up. And here are some more for the road, there's apples, oranges and kiwi"

"For the road?"

"Yeah - It's time to go. People are packin' up, heading home. Vacation time is over"

"Vacation time?"

"Yeah, people nowadays have to schedule a break from their 'real-life' it seems"

"Nowadays?"

"Yes my dear, nowadays." Agnes laughed

Ariara didn't quite grasp the concept of vacation, but before she could ask Agnes to explain more in detail, Etoile came striding up with his suitcase in tow

"Hey you two beautiful creatures... almost ready to leave?"

Ariara looked to Agnes then back at Etoile

"Where are we going?"

"Back home. To the city." He spoke with a sense of irresistible hope in his voice, "If you still have some free days of vacation left, you're more than welcome to stay in my spare room. My place is big. You're in safe hands"

Ariara's heart beat loudly in her chest

Agnes approached, tapped her on the arm and exclaimed, "Good idea! You will get to see one of the oldest cities in the world..."

Oldest cities in the world? She wondered which world she was even in

Agnes continued, "Go with Etoile. Jiemba and I will finish packing up here. He wants to take photos. There's a bridge over an ancient river… We'll meet up with you afterwards, back in the city..."

Ariara hesitated for a moment, but after remembering that she was most likely dreaming, she assented... *go with the flow, what feels good, feels right*

After a warm hug, Agnes waved goodbye. Jiemba put down the bags he was carrying over to his car to join in the sendoff

"My lady..." Etoile said in a carefree, fun loving manner as he opened the front door for Ariara. With his left hand, he signaled for her to get in

She got in enthusiastically, "Thank you, that is nice of you"

Etoile closed her door and she watched him through the front window as he walked to the driver's seat. She stared in awe at the steering wheel, the glove compartment, the complex mechanisms and blinking lights comprising the dashboard

Etoile settled in the driver's seat with confidence

"Buckle up"

Ariara smiled at him, trying to guess what he was talking about

"Oh okay, allow me..." As he reached over and secured her seatbelt, his body drew close. His clean natural manly scent soothed and excited her

He started to drive. There was a brief silence before he said, "I'll just need to call my mother..."

"Call her?"

"Yes. Just to ask her to get the spare room ready for you. And some lunch, I'm sure we'll be hungry by then. She will be so happy to meet you! You'll love her! She's a teacher, her name is Fatima"

Ariara's eyes grew wide as Etoile pulled a little machine out of his pocket and pressed some buttons. *Like Mandana mentioned... How they can communicate from vast distances...*

Whilst Etoile drove and talked to his Mother on the phone, Ariara eased into her seat and observed the houses and scenery passing by. She tried to correlate more of those stories Mandana had told her of Dunya's visions to her current landscape wondering how she even got to this place?

Agnes' face flashed in her mind. *She had made everything seem so familiar and easy*

She was nurturing, welcoming, the way she took care in feeding her and including her into the group touched Ariara deeply. But what was most curious was her uncanny way of answering questions as they formed in her mind...

And how could she have known about the Dragon coin and the oracle?

All of a sudden, Ariara felt her blood rush through her body with a waking flash. *Could Agnes be... Dunya?*

"Is everything alright?" Etoile gently interrupted her musings

"Oh yes, of course. I was just thinking about the wonderful... Vacation!" Ariara smiled proudly to herself for using this new word she had learned so fluidly

"Mother is very excited that you are coming. Be prepared for gifts. She loves to give gifts," He laughed warmly

Ariara smiled graciously. Palpably aware of Etoile's presence, she had to say something to break the tension, "So, how do you know Agnes?"

"Jiemba. I met Agnes through him. He said he just met her recently, but they've really been hitting it off. She's so much fun. Jiemba is a good friend of my mother. I called him uncle growing up"

"That's so funny. He reminds me of my uncle"

"This is your city?!?!" Ariara gasped, her eyes widened, and leaned forward wanting to see it all at once

"Yeah. Here we are! Don't worry, as chaotic as it may seem, we actually have a bit of organization, *system* as we call it"

"No, it's not that. I'm not worried at all, just surprised.

Everyone is moving so fast!!"

"Just a typical busy day. Now you can see why I like to take my vacation at the Mount. A bit of refuge"

They arrived to find Fatima waiting for them at the main entry of the city with some welcome gifts for Ariara, just as Etoile had said she would be

"Mother, I'd like you to meet Ariara," Etoile made the introductions as he kissed Fatima on the forehead

"Welcome to our city! I'm Fatima. It's a pleasure to have you dear. I'm glad my boy called earlier. Here, I got you some stuff for your stay." She handed Ariara a small bag filled with clothes, towels and ladies' essentials, "If you need anything else, don't hesitate to tell me, alright?"

"Oh wow. Thank you. That's very kind of you! Such a beautiful city this is!"

"Beautiful city… oh yes. Busy… yes, yes! It's easy to get lost when you are new here, but my boy here will never allow that to happen for sure. Just gotta keep your feet and legs strong for walking every day"

Ariara looked around to see merchants busy going to and fro, loading mules with products to be brought to the markets. The mules reminded her of her village on the days the nomadic tribes would visit

Etoile laughed, "Walking is good for the body, exercise is essential." His arm around his mother, squeezing tight

"Alright, alright, I know... Where's Jiemba, and his new acquaintance? I thought they went with you?"

"Ah yes, they stopped off on the way back to take some photos by some historical river"

"Hmm, sounds like Jiemba…"

Etoile, mindful of the pedestrian traffic along their way, reached out to hold Ariara's hand

"Stay close to me… I don't want to lose you"

Ariara followed willingly. She was pleased by his light-hearted, caring nature

He winked, "Fond of me now are you? I told you so..."

She tried to hide her blush, looked away briefly. *If you only knew…*

They walked through side alleys. A couple of torn-up, humble wooden houses caught her attention. She found herself amidst a narrow market of beautiful carpets and leather goods. Soon, they reached the end of the alley and stood before a huge building

"This is my school, dear, the oldest in the city" Fatima said as she waved at some children calling her name

Ariara gushed with admiration. Fatima had a powerful aura, commanding respect and love simultaneously

Fatima listened enthusiastically to Etoile narrating his vacation experience, most vividly describing the night ritual of Earth songs…

"…but the best part of the entire trip," he gazed at Ariara, "was when I found my Lucky Star"

Ariara blushed. Fatima gave her a loving wink and a smile, "How about you Lucky Star, how did you enjoy the Earth Songs?"

"Oh! Very much!" She closed her eyes for a moment to recollect the rhythm. "I felt like a newborn baby, just being… I forgot my name, my age…. nothing else really mattered but that sublime moment…"

Fatima smiled warmly, "Lucky Star indeed! You are glowing!"

As they hungrily ate Fatima's delicious food, Etoile made plans for his and Ariara's day

"I was thinking of showing you the Tannery, Ariara, after lunch, would you like that?"

"The Tannery?"

The Tannery was a short walk from Fatima's house. Upon arrival, Etoile talked to the shopkeeper for a moment. They

were led up a small staircase to a terrace

"Ew, what's that smell?"

"Welcome to the Tannery! Nowhere else in the world smells quite like it" The man joked and pointed down to the pits at large stone vessels filled with dyes for making leather goods, "Look, colorful sight, eh? This is one of the oldest tanneries in the world... built thousands of years ago..."

"Yeah, yeah, so we heard! Thanks man, will see you later back at the shop" Etoile dismissed the shopkeeper, wanting Ariara's attention wholly on himself

"He's a talkative one, isn't he?" Etoile laughed as he handed Ariara some fresh mint leaves, "Here, have some of these. Your nostrils will thank you" He sniffed a few of his own as he handed her some

She laughed suddenly at the memory of Mandana, often coming by for mint, feigning a tummy ache in order to have a little chat

"I'm happy to see you laughing, but don't know what's funny about mint leaves"

"Mint leaves remind me of a friend back in my village…"

She stopped short, realizing that she wasn't prepared to tell Etoile anything about her life yet, "I love mint, I use it as a hair rinse, a breath freshener…"

"Oh yeah? Let me see if that works…"

Etoile stole a kiss from her

Naughty! She was frozen yet immediately melted by his kiss

The view from the terrace was exhilarating… *Etoile…* Every word he said, and every move he made, pleased her, made her heart smile

The following morning she found herself with Etoile. They were sitting at the breakfast table discussing the day's plan, a camel ride to watch the sunset, when suddenly there was a knock on the door

It was Jiemba. Dark circles surrounded his teary eyes. Something was obviously wrong

Etoile jumped to attention, comforting his friend. "Come in… is everything okay? Have a seat. I'll get you tea"

Jiemba sat, received the cup of tea from Etoile with shaky hands and gave a weak 'thank you'

He began his story, stopping often to hold back sobs. Ariara wondered why Agnes wasn't with him, but couldn't yet bring herself to ask. Concerned, she hung on every word

"We drove to the riverside just like we had planned… such a glorious sunny day… everything was perfect… oh, my angel…"

He took a moment to compose his thoughts

"We parked the car. Walked hand in hand by the riverside… it was so quiet... birds singing and the rustling sound of leaves on the trees… mystical… smoggy… a bit eerie, so captivating I couldn't stop taking photos. We got to the old bridge I was wanting to see…"

Ariara was shocked at what she saw next. Out of a small envelope, Jiemba pulled a photo out to show them. *Was that painted by a machine? Unbelievable!*

Agnes stood majestically on the bridge, looking afar, deep in thought, lovely, angelic indeed

Jiemba sorrowfully continued, "Then she insisted that she take my photo too. I handed her the camera. When I was on my way up to the bridge, It was like I heard her voice in my head saying *'Thank you for a wonderful experience...'* then I felt some sort of weird feeling of timelessness and disorientation. I felt dizzy... must have blacked out. I have no idea how long for... When I woke up the camera was in my hands and my angel was gone"

"Gone?"

"Of course I checked the river first, but it was just a little shallow stream where we were... Look at the photo! She didn't fall in or... how could she give me the camera back if she fell in the water? I rushed to find some people that we had passed by near the river. I came upon a young couple having a picnic... 'have you seen the woman that was with me' they said that they thought I was alone when they saw me the first time. They 'hadn't noticed' a woman. They looked at me like I was crazy"

"Did you alert the authorities?" Etoile asked, earnestly

"Of course! But I made the mistake of telling them the truth. They probably thought I was drunk or something. I don't even know her real name! They told me that they'll keep an eye out for her - but there's nothing they can really do. I waited and waited... stayed by the riverside overnight... hoping for her to come back... Then I drove back to the city, straight here... I can't believe I lost her"

Ariara, trying to piece things together, couldn't contain her curiosity, "How did you first meet her?"

"Here, in the city. I was walking around taking photos. She just kind of appeared, mystically, wearing a white silk dress... wandering... She never even told me her real name. I called her Agnes, my angel. She went along with it. She didn't share much about herself, so elusive and carefree." Jiemba couldn't help but cry, trying to suppress it, both hands covered his face, "I don't know where to find her..."

Etoile sat near to him, put his arms around him, comforting him

Ariara sat quietly, in deep thought

If she loved Jiemba, why wouldn't she have prepared him for this? How would she know when it's time? How could she...

Her thoughts returned to Etoile... *What if this wonderful time with him is going to end soon? Is this a dream? Am I going to vanish too? This time has felt so magical. If I open up, it may just end abruptly and we will both be devastated...*

Jiemba's voice interrupted her mind's search for answers, "I'll be heading back to the Mount, to see if she went back there..."

"Maybe you should go home to rest first," Etoile suggested

"I can't rest! Not until I find her!"

"Well then, I will come help you search"

Jiemba shook off Etoile's promise of assistance, "No... I need to find her myself. I'm sure she had a reason. I just need to be alone now"

"Alright. I understand. But if you need something along the way, or if you get stuck somewhere, please call me, alright?"

Once Jiemba had gone, Etoile resumed packing for the trip

"I'm quite worried about him going back to the Mount on his own, but I know I couldn't convince him. No one can. He does what he does"

On the road, radio on... Ariara's thoughts wandered once again to Agnes... *or is it Dunya? Did she know it was her time to go? Where did she go?*

She heard her voice echoing, 'Be free. Tomorrow will take care of itself'

"Is everything okay? I wonder what's running through your lovely mind" Etoile prodded gently

She turned her gaze to Etoile and felt a pressure within, squeezing her chest

"I was just thinking about Jiemba... and Agnes"

"He's always involved in some intrigue or another. I'm sure he will find her"

She anxiously opened up her cinch pouch to look for her Dragon coin and was astonished to find a feather from Agnes' headdress...

'Be free'

They arrived at the sand dunes. Ariara shielded her eyes from the blazing sun and marveled at the vast golden hills set against the searing blue cloudless sky

Etoile marveled with her as he opened the door. "The Camel Boy's name is Salem. He's quite a character. Unfortunately, he can't speak, but he is the best guide"

As soon as they got out of the car, Salem ran towards them. At first, he gestured wildly, communicating his excitement. Then he blushed, star-struck, upon first laying eyes on Ariara. He gave her a welcoming gentleman's bow. Etoile patted him heartily on the back and signaled a quick introduction

Salem guided them to the two camels prepared for their sunset sand dunes ride. He communicated enthusiastically, the best way he could... signaled *"three"* with his fingers and mimed the marching motion of a soldier

"He's saying there are three easy steps to riding a camel," Etoile chuckled

Of course, Ariara had plenty of camel riding experience, but she felt it was only polite to play along. Also, she wasn't sure how she would explain that village experience to Etoile

"Alright, I'll try my best. Three easy steps you say? I hope I can get it right?"

Salem bade one of the camels to sit on the sand. He climbed onto its back, grabbed the saddle's handlebars, and held with a very firm grip. As the camel slowly stood up, Salem gracefully actioned to sway with the camel, in three motions, 'back-front-back', until the camel was in full standing position

Salem dismounted from the Camel, showing off his agility to Ariara in the process. Back on the ground he swayed his body in slow motion, his hands holding onto imaginary handlebars

"Hold the bars firmly and sway with the camel, never go against it" Etoile chimed in

They travelled with the camel caravan through the desert sands en route to the desert camp for almost an hour. Ariara felt majestic riding on the huge yet very gentle creature. They reached the camp, dismounted, and stretched their bodies

Salem's fondness for Ariara was obvious. Though she couldn't understand most of what he was signaling, he engaged her in a long, deep, sign language conversation. As he gesticulated with vivid intensity, she nodded and smiled politely… *I wonder what he's trying to tell me*

He beamed whilst preparing the carpet so she could sit on the sand. She smiled appreciatively at this gesture and gladly sat

All of a sudden, he tugged at the carpet, pulling her along for a short ride. Ariara was surprised, scared, shouted, and ended up rolling off into the hot sand, upside down and laughing

After Etoile was sure that she wasn't injured, he couldn't help laughing. Ariara playfully punched him in his arm

They walked a few steps up the dune. Salem prepared the carpet again for Ariara to sit, this time, comfortably

"Please, not another slide ride!!!"

"*No*" Salem shook his head, then sat directly beside Ariara, leaving Etoile no room on the carpet to sit

"Looks like I've been replaced," Etoile teased, they laughed as he squeezed his way on, slyly putting his arm around Ariara as he sat

The quiet desert… the sunset… heavenly… I can't think of anywhere else I'd rather be than here with you, now

As the sun split the horizon, Etoile reached for her hand, "Told you it was glorious here"

"Absolutely"

She leaned her head on his shoulder. They sat quietly till the sun was fully set

After, Salem led them to the tent arranged for their night's stay. It was time for him to bid farewell but it was overtly obvious that he wanted to spend more time with Ariara. Etoile teased her as she gave him a hug and kissed his forehead in gratitude

Salem pulled an hourglass filled with desert sand from his pocket as a gift for her. He placed it in her hand, drew it near his heart

"Aww. Thank you for today, and for this. You are such a dear. I'll never forget, yes… I'll never forget you"

Etoile walked with Salem a few steps on the way out of the camp, talked and had some sort of exchange that escaped Ariara's eye

They chatted by a bonfire, under the bright desert moon, Etoile teasing Ariara about Salem's affinity for her

"He gave you quite a gift"

Ariara took the hourglass from her bag and held it up so they could both look at it against the backdrop of the fire and night sky

"He normally sells those to tourists for a pretty penny. I tried to pay him for it but he refused. Told me it was his personal gift to you. You stole the Best Camel Boy's heart! How do you do this, huh?"

"Do what? Ride a camel? I just followed the three easy

steps" She replied shyly, feigning naivete

Etoile reached into his pocket and pulled out a little clay pot "Salem's personal gift to you?" She asked in fun

"Close your eyes..."

Willingly. Eyes closed, she heard Etoile softly clacking the small pot

"I got you something, too. Want to guess?"

"Hmm... tell me"

"Just guess... first thing that comes to mind"

Her head raised up with still closed eyes, trying to catch a word from the desert skies

A star...

"Now, open your eyes..." Etoile opened the little pot revealing a charm... "For my Lucky Star"

It reminded her of the darkest nights back in the village, stars twinkling in the skies. She held the little pot, gently picked up the bronze Star charm… a perfect addition to her cinch pouch

"I love it!" She held his hand, opened his left palm, and traced his strong palm lines, also forming a Star… *are you my Star?* She held back speaking anything about his palm lines, instead she held his hand a while longer, "Thank you for this. I truly love it"

Before she was able to put her new trinket into her cinch pouch, he moved closer to her

"Let's make a wish"

Etoile gently traced her hairline from her forehead down to her neck. His gaze was tender, drawing her in. He touched her cheek, her heart pumping as his lips softly brushed hers…

Ariara's body lay still, eyes closed

Suddenly, her nose started to itch, left cheek began to twitch

She slowly opened her eyes, only to see, through the brightness of the Sun's rays - a boy with a small twig of laurel leaves in his hand, brushing them lightly on her face

"Hey, what are you doing?" Ariara said softly, and with her eyes struggling against the light of the Sun, gently signaled for him to stop

"Ahh... finally you are awake," the boy sat back with a sigh of relief

She rubbed her eyes. *Awake? How long have I been asleep?*

The boy shrugged as he pointed to the remains of a bonfire, "I found you here last night... The fire was out, you were all alone. I started a new one and covered you with that wool blanket..."

Why am I naked? Am I home? back in Love Valley? How did I...? Where did I...? The sunset, sands, desert night, Etoile... She noticed her clothes folded beside her. The night of her last moon ritual flashed in her mind

The boy seemed concerned, "Are you alright?"

She tried to gain composure as she answered, "I think so.... Thank you for keeping me safe... My name is Ariara…"

"I know who you are. You're the Governor's niece, with the beautiful garden"

"Thank you.... And you? What's your name?"

"Aries"

"The shepherd's boy?"

He cleared his throat and put his hands on his hips, "Well, I consider myself a young man, not a boy. But yes, my father is a shepherd…"

Ariara blinked and shielded her eyes from the bright sun as Aries' continued, excitedly, "I'm so happy that I'm finally meeting you. I want to ask you so many questions about your garden... but I need to get back home now. My parents might be worried. Can I walk you back to the village?"

"Sure, sure, ok... Give me a few moments to get dressed… Please, turn around"

"Of course!!" He turned his back whilst she put on her clothes

The walk back to the village slowly eased her back to her familiar reality, but the abrupt end to her enchanted experience with Etoile upset her. The realization that it was just a dream made her heart sink

She walked, bewildered, whilst Aries persisted in talking about her garden, "I want to be a healer too someday. Maybe I can come by and help you?"

"Sure. Why not..."

"Really?!?! Thank you!! I can lift heavy things. That's no problem for me. And I don't mind sweeping the floor..."

Ariara was too exasperated to ask him any questions about Dunya, but she kept it tucked in the back of her mind for future reference

Back in her cave, her things were placed in the same order she left them in. Jars untouched. She wondered... *Has anyone noticed I was gone? How will I explain when even I don't understand.... How long was I gone?*

It was afternoon when she decided to visit Mandana

"Hello Mandana, are you there?"

"Oh, Ariara? Is that you? Come on in, dear…" Mandana answered, putting aside a thick journal she was writing in

"How are you feeling today?" Ariara gave her a firm, tight, and loving hug

"Oh, oh… I'm alright," She laughed, surprised by the sudden warm embrace, "What happened? Did you really miss me that much?"

"I just came by to say hi, and to check on you. Did the mint help your tummy ache?"

"Actually, I knocked on your door three days ago. It worked very well, but, you know how my stomach is… Wanted to ask you for some more. Figured you went away on a trip. Haven't seen you"

So… just three days

"Oh yeah… I did, umm…. And I just so happened to bring some more mint leaves with me, just in case…"

As she handed Mandana the fragrant mint leaves, she thought of Etoile at the terrace, his charming smile, his stolen kiss

"Well, thank you for thinking of me dear." Mandana couldn't help but notice Ariara smitten. "Tell me, where did you go on your trip?"

"Ah, it wasn't really a trip. I was just… gathering herbs in Love Valley" she smiled, as more memories of Etoile at the terrace flooded her mind

She barely remembered leaving Mandana's. Her mind was too flooded with dreamy memories. She hoped she had said her goodbyes politely

Part II

Lethargy subsumed Ariara since her reawakening in the valley. She shut herself up in her cave for days. Her mind spun, non-stop. Reliving the illusions brought her delight and misery all at once... *But if It was just a dream, why do I still feel this deep connection to Etoile? Why do I still long for him?*

She had completely forgotten her promise to Aries, and was surprised when he showed up at her cave for his first gardening lesson

It was tempting to ask him what he remembered about Dunya, but he was so eager to jump into action, that she just tucked it into the back of her mind and focused on the tasks at hand. *A beneficial distraction...*

One pleasant day, after walking Aries home, Ariara passed by her favorite row of apple trees. A short distance ahead was a small hill on which an Oak tree majestically stood. It looked as if to be keeping watch over the valley. *How have I not noticed that tree before?*

She climbed up the hill. A steady and very gentle breeze filled the air. Serenity enveloped her as she approached the tree. A hollow in its trunk formed a gentle abode, a grounded nest, a place of rest for those who sought one. The sense of endurance the Oak tree exuded gave her comfort

Amidst the storms you gloriously stand

She felt sensually drawn to take refuge in the hollow. She sat in, cross legged, settling her entire body into the Oak tree's embrace. In the sacred caress of the mighty Oak, she peered out to a panorama of the valley

As she sunk into her quiet zone, an inner anguish came to a crest. Pangs for Etoile rose, raw, crushing her being. She closed her eyes, and the tormenting truth unraveled... *Falling for someone, connecting deeply, only for that experience to end at any instant. What then is love for? Was it love? What is love?*

Her questions remained unanswered. Her eyes remained closed tightly, sorrow pouring out in a flood of unrestrainable tears. This moment allowed her to open up, all emotions irresistibly felt... Longing. Hunger... Questioned thoroughly, until she was consumed, spent, empty. Then, there in that emptiness she was left with the humbling acceptance that she never had control to begin with

I can't know, until I know what Love means to me

The Oak tree had her back, her stronghold. She embraced the desire to stand amidst the storms. She opened her eyes... the Love Valley. Still a magnificent, lovely sight

Before heading home, she picked up a small oak twig, into her cinch pouch

Ariara sat by her window, looking out. It was a full

moon once again

'Good night,' the valley whispered serenely...

She prepared for bed. When she opened her blanket, her pouch flew open. Her trinkets scattered. Holding her lamp, she knelt down and gathered them one by one... Her oak twig, stones, dragon coin, feather, hourglass... She opened the little clay pot and found her charm... The Star...

Etoile's voice carried in the wind...

"Make a wish..."

A solemn tear fell down her cheek, "I wish you were here..."

The delightful smell of fragrant herbs permeated the air. Flowers in bloom, exquisite rows of blue tulips, set to music by the enchanting sounds of nature

Seven months had passed since that afternoon when she

found solace in the Oak tree. She spent most of her time tending to her garden, learning how best to plant seeds, cultivate soil, and nourish young buds. Her appreciation of this symbiotic process grew; from nurturing, to blossoming, to a healthy harvest picking. She found profound pleasure in crafting her herbs into medicinal tinctures and ointments. Allowing them, and her, to serve a greater purpose in the village

Whenever memories of Etoile popped up, holding her Star charm assured her... *All is well*...

Aries had become an avid student, helping her with the garden, carrying jars, learning about herbs. His curiosity encouraged her to experiment and gain invaluable insight. One particularly sunny afternoon, she was so immersed in her inner life that she hardly noticed him calling out...

"The nomads have just arrived!"

She smiled and replied gently, "That's great news. Shall we go see what they brought?"

"Yes! We need new jars!! Let's get more colors this time? It would be a lot easier to remember what herb is in which jar if they have colors... I'm not really good at remembering those. When they're wet, they all just look like green leaves to me"

"Genius! What a clever suggestion. I'll let you choose the jars this time, alright"

The nomads arrived in the village with a dozen mules. They were almost finished unpacking and displaying their carpets, blankets, cooking pots, vessels, jars and other stuff on the ground, easy for villagers to browse and shop

Aries was exhilarated as he perused the wide assortment of jars, jumping from one display to another, clutching his empty sack. "We should get this one and this one. Not this one…"

Ariara enjoyed seeing him so exuberant. She followed close behind, giving him approving nods to keep him going

After choosing the perfect jars, she settled payment with the merchant. Aries gleefully filled his sack, but accidentally dropped one small jar. It rolled over towards a carriage where a woman was standing. She picked up the jar and handed it back to him

Aries went to take the jar and thank the woman. When he saw her face, he froze in disbelief...

"D... Dun... Dunya !!!?"

As soon as Ariara heard the name, her eyes darted up to see... Agnes... *Dunya? She's exactly as I remembered... dreamed. Will she recognize me? It was in my dream, no? Would she remember being in the same dream too?*

Aries, still in shock, pointed at her, "It's Dunya! Dunya is back!"

"You remember me? I'm flattered. Well, you have grown into a handsome young man! I'm happy to see you... glad to be back here..." Dunya took a deep breath, relishing the moment

"Dunya... I'm Ariara. I've heard a lot about you... glad to finally meet you... I'm living in your old cave... my uncle..."

"Ariara! I remember you...."

From my dream?

"Your uncle mentioned you fondly, many times. Finally

we meet. I'm Dunya!"

Aries interrupted, tugging on Dunya's sleeve, "Where did you go?! Are you finally back to stay!?"

"Boy, It's a long story, but yes, I'm finally back. How is Mandana?"

Ariara answered, "Cheerful as ever, and... I'm sure she'd be happy to see you!!"

"I was about to pay her a visit. Let's walk together"

When they got to Mandana's cave, she was standing by her entry, seemingly just arriving too, a full fruit basket in hand. When she saw them, she gasped

"Dunya?!?!"

"Mandana!" Dunya ran towards her and hugged her tight, tighter

"Dunya!!! Is this for real? Dunya!!! You are alive! Oh dear, you left without a word! Where have you been? I thought... Come on in. I just got some fresh fruits today, these are definitely meant for us ladies. You have a lot of explaining to do!"

Aries wanted to join the fruit feast, but Ariara reminded him that he needed to put all the new jars away. Mandana sent him on his way with a juicy apple

As they entered her cozy abode, Mandana was overcome with joy, "I feel so blessed!! How did you two ladies end up at my door?"

Dunya laughed, "Oh, you can thank Aries for introducing us. He was the first to welcome me back. Still remembers me!"

"You must have shocked the hell out of that poor boy!"

Dunya suddenly took Mandana's hand, held it tenderly, "I'm really sorry I didn't get to say goodbye to you that day. You must have been..."

"No, no, you've made everything alright by showing up today... But you must tell me, where have you been all this time?!?"

Dunya moved closer and spoke in a hushed tone, like a young girl about to tell a secret

"Well, one afternoon, down in the valley, whilst collecting twigs for my bonfire, I saw a man sitting on the ground engrossed in drawing. I couldn't help but approach him. I saw that he was drawing the Love Valley landscape. I initiated a conversation. He was so focused on his drawing, all he would answer with was 'yes, my angel'. Then he..."

Ariara interrupted, "He called you his angel?"

"Who was this man, my angel? Where is he now?" Mandana prodded, eager to hear more

"His name is... was... Jiemba"

Jiemba??? Ariara's heart raced

"He told me he only had that one day to finish his drawing of the valley. We stayed there till night time. We hit it off, you know. He had more drawings he wanted to show me back at his caravan. Before dawn, we walked there. He owned a carriage and a few mules. We stayed in his carriage, not to be disturbed... before I knew it we were leaving the village and I didn't have the chance to say goodbye"

Mandana suddenly fumed, "A romantic escapade? Dunya!!! We thought you were dead. I thought I would never see you again. I know what you're going to say, you were just …"

"Being free… letting tomorrow take care of itself..." Dunya finished Mandana's sentiment, trying to pacify her, teary eyed

Ariara couldn't help herself. She needed to know, "Where is Jiemba now?"

Dunya's tone grew solemn, "One day, all of a sudden, he changed the tribe's route to set up camp near a river bank. He wanted to draw the landscape. There was a bridge there... For three days and nights, he couldn't stop drawing. Then, when I woke up on the fourth day, he was nowhere to be found. We all frantically looked for him. Some people said they heard some splash sound in the river the night before. He might have drowned. No one knows what happened… I blame myself for not staying beside him that night as he continued to draw…"

Mandana tried to comfort her reunited friend, "I'm so sorry dear"

"You were precious to him," Ariara murmured

Dunya looked at her with surprise

Ariara continued, "You were precious to him. He wouldn't have done anything he thought would lead to losing you." She spoke slowly, carefully choosing her words, hearing echoes of Jiemba's cries from her dream. She couldn't help pursuing the mystery further, "Do you have any of his drawings?"

"Yes, of course. His nephew drives the bigger carriage where Jiemba's stuff is stored. They had to stop by the apothecary for some medicines, and should be here within the next few weeks... I will show you his drawings when they arrive…"

Mandana gave a brief puzzling look to Ariara, then turned back to Dunya, "You need rest! You can stay here with me for as long as you need to"

Ariara spent three full weeks working non-stop in her thriving garden. Aries' curation of colored jars had added a vibrancy that made her heart smile

In these quiet moments alone, she would try to make sense of recent events. Most of all, she tried to make sense of her visions. Her vision of Agnes... Dunya and Jiemba had manifested into reality. Both being devastated by the loss of one another

Could Dunya have known the river was the end? Could she have done something to prevent another painful experience too soon? What exactly does she mean by 'letting tomorrow take care of itself'?

She took a long deep look at her plants, feeling a new appreciation for the symbiotic uniqueness of every stem and petal, the collective collage of color and fragrance

All is well...

It was past noon when Ariara left her garden. She had a quick bite, and went for a walk

The entire village is taking a nap. No one seems to be in any pain or having bodily aches today... A healthy village means more quiet moments for me

She headed up the hill to her Oak tree. Sitting comfortably cross legged, she breathed in... and out...

At a distance, the Love Valley... She noticed two people strolling by

Dunya... and uncle?

She was unprepared for what followed. The Governor and Dunya embraced, then passionately kissed

Shocked by what she saw, she stood up and walked hurriedly back down to the village. Immediately, she was greeted by an excited Aries

"Another caravan has arrived, wanna check on it before it gets dark?"

She spoke evenly, trying to maintain her calm, "Alright, now you've become the village's official caravan arrival alert. Let's go!"

Dunya had somehow arrived to greet the caravan at the exact same time. The Governor was not with her. She waved Ariara and Aries over

Ariara lowered her head, hoping that she hadn't been noticed

Dunya grabbed her hand and led her towards an arriving carriage, "You're just in time! He's here!! Jiemba's nephew!"

Suddenly, Etoile's voice rang in Ariara's ears, '*He's a good friend of my mother. I called him uncle growing up...*'

Could this be Etoile? Is my own vision coming to fruition?

Her heart beat like never before. Her hands grew cold, her knees weak, but she continued towards the carriage, and stood next to Dunya

Out of the carriage stepped a handsome, dark haired man with a familiar smile. The smile that made her forget all else in the world...

"Etoile..." she murmured, her eyes open wide, her body stock-still, petrified

"You know him?" Aries nudged her. She remained frozen

The man took a hurried stride towards Dunya and hugged her tight. "Oh Dunya, I'm sorry I couldn't come sooner, our route was delayed..."

Tears flowed from her eyes, "I'm sure he's drawing now. Wherever he is"

"I have all his drawing sheets in the carriage. I'm sure he'd want you to have them"

They relaxed their embrace. As he extended his arm to point back to the carriage, he cringed in obvious pain

"Are you okay? What's wrong?" Dunya asked

"I must have eaten something bad. Don't worry, I have medicine..."

Dunya regained her poise and noticed Ariara standing next to her, "Oh, I'm sorry, where are my manners? This is Ariara, the governor's niece"

"Hello Ariara. I'm Wadjuri. Glad to meet you"

He extended his arm for a friendly handshake, that familiar smile on his face... His gaze fleeting, still trying to relieve some pain from his lower torso

"Et... Wa...djuri??" Ariara was shocked. *No...your name is Etoile...*

"...and this is my Beloved, Bituin" Wadjuri stepped back after the short introduction and assisted Bituin down the carriage, kissing her cheekily on the neck

Aries took the chance to introduce himself, "I'm Aries! Welcome to our village!"

"He's our official caravan arrival alert..." Ariara tried to sound as unnerved as possible

Dunya tapped Aries on the shoulder, "Come, help me get Jiemba's drawing box... Let's all go to my place. You can comfortably stretch and have some rest"

Ariara said very little. She was in a state of shock, trying to process all that had happened today. First, seeing Dunya and her uncle together in the Love Valley, then seemingly reuniting with Etoile, only to find out that his name is Wadjuri and he doesn't recognize her. To top it all, he has a beloved

Dunya's new cave was sparsely furnished, but comfortable. Wadjuri and Bituin sat beside each other at a small table. Dunya offered them some bread and fruits. Wadjuri ate very little. He seemed fatigued and in pain. Still, he tended to Bituin. She looked at him lovingly

So, what was that vision all about then? I wished for him to be here. Here he is. He looks exactly like Etoile, his smile, his build, his mannerisms. Except... he doesn't recognize me...How dare he call me his Lucky Star...I wished for you to be here. But not in this way. It hurts...

Dunya opened Jiemba's box. She handed several sketches to Ariara. Aries joined in the spontaneous gallery viewing

"Wow. There's... a lot!" Ariara tried her best to sound enthused

"I'm glad I have these memories of him, the world through his eyes. Here, look, this is the river I was telling you about"

There it was. The drawing of Agnes on the bridge over the river was exactly as she remembered from her vision, Jiemba's machine painting

Flooded with emotion, her body felt weak. She took a few

deep breaths before finding comforting words for Dunya

"He was always true to you"

"Yes. I know he loved me, as much as I love him"

What does Love mean to you? Are you also 'in love' with my uncle? Is that how you 'let tomorrow take care of itself'?

Ariara stood up, more abruptly than she would have liked to

I need to go home

She faced Wadjuri and Bituin, but hardly looked at them. "I'm sorry, I need to attend to some work in my garden. It was a pleasure meeting you both. Enjoy your stay. If you need any herbs, just reach out. I'm a few doors away"

Bituin stood up in appreciation, "Wadjuri has been feeling ill. We have some medicines here but if none of these work, we'll come see you"

"Yes! Please don't hesitate"

Ariara barely slept, woke up tired, stayed in bed for a while. She tried to build up energy to carry her through the day, shunting off yesterday's events from her mind

Why doesn't my vision align with reality? Dunya and Jiemba came true, why not... Why isn't he Etoile? Nothing makes sense... Am I losing myself?

No. I have a Life to Live... Today... Stay Present, Ariara!

After breakfast, she walked along the village's main road distributing herbs, engaging in some light friendly chatter along the way. She tried to be present in her interactions by spending quality time with the villagers. They showed their appreciation for her presence by giving her fresh fruits, delicious bread, and lovely flowers

She ran into Mandana at the village centre, dressed in her usual rugged attire and wearing a wide straw hat

"Hi Mandana. What are you up to today?"

"Ariara! I stopped by your cave earlier... I'm glad I found you here. I saw Dunya, She told me that Jiemba's nephew and his... companion have arrived"

"Ah, yes I met them last night." Eager to change the topic, she showed Mandana the gifts she had received. "Look what I got! Delivered some herbs today... Wasn't expecting such lovely gifts but they insisted I take them!"

"Well you know when you show up with love, you get love right back. All the villagers are so blessed by your passion..."

Love??? Mandana's always occupied with the other villagers' lives... babies being born, birthdays, weddings, but... I've never noticed Mandana being... in love...What does Love mean to Mandana?

"Did I lose you there somewhere?" she giggled

"Yeah, slightly. Interesting thought. You may need to tell me more about that..." Ariara disguised her confusion with a chuckle

"Before that, I wanted to ask you to help me plant these seeds"

"What seeds?"

"You know the apple trees on the village roadside? I

planted those back in the days…"

"Wow! I love those trees!"

She had grown accustomed to strolling on that trail. Not just for the beautiful view of the Love Valley, but also for the gorgeous shade those young trees gave, especially mid afternoon, when the sun was blazing high

"Yeah. All of them. Not in one day of course… I plant trees whenever I feel the need to 'plant' my thoughts, my feelings, my choices... whatever comes up. It's been a tremendous help for me at some difficult points in my life. I was thinking we could plant some together this time"

"And, what are we 'planting' for this time?"

"Well let's go and find out, shall we?"

Mid-day when the sun was still high, they joyfully dug a hole for the first tree

"Mandana, I know so little bit about Dunya... I'm curious"

"Ha. Aren't we all?"

Ariara couldn't help confiding in Mandana, "I saw her with my uncle in Love Valley a few days back"

"Ah, well, you know, she's been gone for years. Perhaps he wanted... you know, old friends catching up"

"Hmm... Old friends"

Although Mandana talks to everyone, she was no bee buzzing amongst flowers. She looked at Ariara, waiting for her to ask more questions...

Ariara tactfully continued, "How did you get to be so close to my uncle?"

"I used to work in his registry. You know, villagers come to him with problems, concerns, gifts..."

"Ah! No wonder you know everyone in the village"

Mandana laughed softly, "Yes, even after I left the registry, people would come to my cave to chat. I enjoy the conversation. I really don't mind. Much like how you enjoy your garden and giving out herbs to people in need"

"Hmm… yeah, I guess so…." She paused, "Mandana, you mentioned 'Love' before… Have you ever been in love?"

"Of course dear"

"Tell me about your experience, please"

Mandana smiled, reminiscing, "Ahh… he used to bring me fruits and flowers… We'd talk about everything under the sun… I melted in his tender, loving gaze... His voice…"

Ariara, as if in a trance, began to recount some of her own memories of Etoile, "... the sands, the desert, the starry night, those kisses…"

Mandana laughed, "Ohh sands and deserts? Lovely setting! Where are we now dear?"

Ariara caught herself, "Just seeing beyond what's in front of us." She fixed her stare afar, showing a soft smile on her right cheek

"Of course! Carry on! I love seeing what's beyond here

too. I feel you have that in you dear"

"What do I have?"

"That sense of knowing. Moving deeper. I'm sure you must have visionary dreams too. That's why you were so curious about Dunya and her sketchings. You also seem to have that same habit of sleeping under the full moon... I admire you both for it. That dreamy side... "

"Oh, we can talk about me and Dunya next time. I wanna hear more about you. Do... did you love him?"

"I do"

"What happened then?"

"Well he expressed his interest in me, and I told him..." She paused, re-living feelings once felt, "Let's take a break. I need some water. Want some? Maybe we can get a better glimpse of those sands and deserts from over there"

They both laughed as they moved to sit on a nearby stone bench. Mandana wiped her brow. Ariara took a sip of cool water and waited quietly

Mandana continued, "We understand Love as we experience it. This journey we take can be thrilling or tormenting, based on the choices we make and how we act, or cope, once those choices are made. Falling in love is like getting into a maze where there is no map to follow. But once you're in, you get to choose how you want to experience finding your way around"

"Woh-woh! Slow down Mandana! I'm losing sight of the beautiful sands of the desert"

Mandana grew more tender and held Ariara's hand warmly, "Never be afraid to lose sight of the beautiful sands..."

"But, I don't want to lose sight... It feels good to be in..."

"Of course, I know it feels good. Especially with all the loving gaze, charming smile, kisses, yaa yaa yaa... But, no one can survive in those beautiful desert sands without water. You need to find a fertile spot that thrives. You need to find an oasis to survive"

"An Oasis? How do I find it?"

Mandana paused for a moment as she reflected, "By knowing what you are willing to commit to. Each of us has to find our own path to our own oasis. Success in finding that path mostly depends on commitment to finding it, and then tending to it... no matter the obstacles"

Ariara stood and stretched, allowing air to flow through her body as she took a deep breath. "Mandana, you sound so sure about these things. Have you always been certain..."

All of a sudden, they heard a frantic voice calling out. Dunya ran towards them, "We need your help! It's Wadjuri! He's gotten worse..."

Ariara's heart raced when she heard his name. She stopped home to quickly gather together some herbal remedies and rushed over to Dunya's cave

Wadjuri was in bed, under a blanket, warm cloths on his forehead and wrapped around his feet. He was shivering, lips dry, pale face, eyes closed. Bituin sat with him, wiping his brow

"He's been having this pain for months now. We packed medicine from his family's alchemist. That was supposed to be good for this journey, but it seems like they haven't helped. He's gotten much worse today…"

Ariara tried to keep it together as this abrupt incident vertiginously unraveled. Wadjuri's anguish pierced her heart. Her eyes welled with tears she held back. She struggled inside to get her composure back, kept her emotions suppressed, her words unspoken. Despite a wretched inner monologue she calmly stayed present within the rhythm of reality unfolding

She searched through her satchel and sat next to him. She began to put some herbal oil on his forehead, arms, chest, torso, legs, feet

The hours passed in torment. This charming man who starred in her rhapsody all these months now lay before her, inanimate, lifeless

Midnight. Dunya's cave was warm but Wadjuri shivered beneath heavy blankets. His eyes rolled when opened. He kept them shut in pain

Bituin beside Dunya, wailed and waited, hoping for Wadjuri to get through this suffering. Mandana murmured prayers for safe passage - for his human body's pain to subside

Ariara continued to rub soothing oils on his body, keeping him warm. She longed to tell him about her vision but held back. *Not with Bituin weeping beside him*

Wadjuri's shivering slowed. His eyes, half shut. Gradually letting go of fighting pain. Bituin cried harder. Ariara's eyes welled with tears as she reached for his face and closed his eyelids

He took his last deep breath... and released

It was three hours past midnight

Wadjuri's body was wrapped in cloths and brought to the carriage. Bituin wept. The carriage men solemnly prepared for their departure

Dunya whispered to Mandana, "I'm going with Bitiun to bring him to his family. His mother will be devastated. She never approved of him going with the tribes due to his poor health, but he chose to roam, like Jiemba"

"May the Divine bless his soul wherever he goes from here"

"Oh Mandana... I seem to be the bearer of bad news" Dunya was teary-eyed hoping for her friend's comforting words

"Shhh, nah... Don't think that way"

"I feel like I just got back. I wanted to stay here, my home.... but I feel obliged..."

Mandana couldn't help but shed tears. "I was just getting used to seeing you again... But, this is your journey. You'll get through it the way you always do... take care of yourself, Dunya"

They hugged each other tight

Dunya turned her attention to Ariara. She had barely moved, and not spoken a single word, since Wadjuri's departure

"Thank you Ariara for helping him ease through his suffering. I'll tell his mother you were all there for him"

They shared a quick, tight, hug before Dunya joined Bituin in the carriage and they bid farewell

Goodbye

They sat quietly for a while as Mandana boiled water for tea. She took her first bite of an apple and sighed. Ariara took a piece of bread. She chewed, and broke into tears

"Ariara my dear..."

Mandana sat on the hassock beside her

"Remember when you asked me if I have visionary dreams like Dunya... I had one. It was when I fell asleep in the Valley... I saw Dunya. This was before she came back. I didn't know it was her at first..."

"Really? Exactly Dunya?"

"Exactly! Her face, her body, her voice, her easy going attitude. And I met Jiemba too. He even showed me a machine painting of that same river with the same bridge where they got separated… When Wadjuri came with Jiemba's drawing box and I saw his drawings, it was the same bridge"

Ariara took another sip and straightened her back

"And... Then there was Etoile... He arranged for the best Camel boy, Salem! We rode over sand dunes to watch the sunset... spent a glorious night in the desert. We had... the best night... and then…"

"Ah, so that's where those beautiful sands of the desert came from. Go on..."

"It just ended! Mandana! It all felt so real to my bones. His voice still carried in the wind for months. Those dark nights I wouldn't want to go through again… and these last few days have been the zenith of torture… Wadjuri looked exactly like Etoile in my vision! Why? Why did he have to show up here with another woman, another name... and fate had me witness his last painful hours. I feel so hopeless... Why? Why??""

She looked down and burst into more tears. Mandana consoled her

"What's important is what you appreciated about, not just that, but learned most from that experience. Let me ask you, what did you learn about yourself?"

"It was just a dream. What does it matter?"

"Of course it matters. It's part of your life, your journey. What did you learn about yourself?"

"Well, now I know that I'm capable of jumping into a wagon with someone from a spur of the moment desire. But, my instincts were right. Etoile… He was kind and considerate of my well being"

"That's important"

"How am I gonna get through this, Mandana?"

"Have you looked more closely at the tapestry on your wall? The one I wove for Dunya? The tapestry that covered up her sketchings…"

"Not really. Sorry… Why?

"I wove a wheel of life on there"

"A wheel of life?"

Before Mandana could explain further, they were both jolted by knocking at the door

"Mandana! Mandana..."

Before Mandana could reply, the governor dashed inside. He was frazzled, "Ariara? What are you doing here?"

Mandana answered for her, "Dunya's friend passed away last night. Ariara was up all night tending to him..."

"Dunya? Where is she now?"

"She just left to bring his body back to his family"

"What? She left... Again?" his voice was charged with disgust...

Ariara stood up, "I'll leave you to talk. Uncle, it seems like you have some urgent matter..."

The Governor handed Mandana an envelope, "I will come back. I'm going to walk Ariara home"

Mandana was on the verge of tears. She nodded quietly

He walked with his head down. Ariara was already exhausted, she braced herself for the bad news that she felt was coming

"Your Aunt has passed away, Ariara. She went peacefully. In her sleep"

Ariara softly wept as they walked slowly towards her cave. The Governor continued to speak gently, yet Ariara could sense he was stricken deeply by grief

"She was very fond of you. Proud of how you've brought your beautiful way with herbs to the village. When you approached us after your mother left, I was unsure if it was a good idea for you to come live here. I thought you'd be happier eventually in your own village. I thought that you just wanted to come here to escape the pain of feeling abandoned... I'm sorry, I'm saying too much..."

"No, Uncle, please, I want to hear..."

"It was your Aunt who convinced me to bring you into our

village... It was the right decision. One we've never regretted. You brighten up the village.... I just want you to know that your Aunt was very proud of you. We both are"

Tears flowed down her cheeks. She stared at her uncle wondering how he feels now that aunt is gone... *are you also happy now that you and Dunya are free?*

A cold breeze swept through as Mandana and Ariara laid flowers on the tomb of Mithraia

Tears flowed down Mandana's cheeks, "Sorry it had to end this way... may you rest in peace." She turned to console Ariara, also weeping, "She was a kind, gentle, loving person. She loved your uncle so much"

"Uncle loved her too... right?"

"Of course"

Ariara gently rubbed Mandana's back as tears continued to flow down both of their cheeks

"I wish I had spent more time with her"

Before heading back they both said prayers for her soul... *may she find peace wherever she goes*

They reached the village roadside where apple trees gave them shade as they walked by. Mandana looked up and smiled in appreciation

Ariara gripped Mandana's hand tightly. She couldn't keep her secret any longer, "I saw uncle kissing Dunya in the Love Valley..."

Mandana stopped for a moment

"Ariara... Your uncle and aunt grew apart after they found out they couldn't have a child together..."

A moment of silence passed between them, then Mandana continued

"After I no longer worked at the registry, your uncle would visit me to talk. He would pour out his frustrations in life. It became his usual routine. Talking about things made him feel better, less intense in his reactions to his day's challenges. One night he visited me at the same time Dunya came by to talk about her visionary dreams. I told you before, he was fascinated by her stories. Dunya invited him to join her in her walks to the valleys... I guess they found they had similar views in their approach to life"

"Why would Aunt stay married to him?"

"Only she would know what was in her heart"

As they continued to walk by the roadside, Mandana spotted a familiar hill

"Ariara, let's walk up that hill. It's been a while since I've gone up there"

She was silently pleased at Mandana's suggestion. That was the hill that held her fortress - the Oak tree which gave her the strength to endure walking down the path of finding herself once again...

They reached the hilltop. Restfully, they sat under the Oak tree facing the entire landscape of the Love Valley

Mandana spoke softly through tears, "It's all part of experience... process... after planting all those apple trees... under the blazing sun... this hill was a private place to cry on and shout my pain away. I came here to rest in the arms of this Oak tree...This hill welcomed me without judgement when I was at my lowest moments... the sole witness of my ultimate cries"

"This Oak tree? Oh Mandana! I've cried here too!!"

Mandana looked at her intently. Her eyes welled with tears. They shared a long hug. Mandana picked up an acorn and handed it to her. She leaned her head on her shoulder in gratitude. She placed the acorn into her cinch pouch...

Finding a familiar soul is a moment worth remembering

Ariara spoke after a bit, "Well, I've been thinking about who I'd like to share my Oasis with... Someone with a charming smile..."

"What else?"

"Someone I can trust to consider my well being in his thoughts and actions as much as I would for him, and we work together to grow and flourish"

"That's a good start! Knowing that makes it a little easier to act and react to circumstances presented to you along the way"

"In the meantime I will continue to do what I love to do, tend to my garden"

"Now you're learning! And - don't worry about the trees. I got that covered!"

They both laughed, got up together, and walked joyfully

Part III

Aries' gaiety and companionship had kept her present. In the weeks gone by since her aunt passed away, Ariara hadn't seen much of her uncle. She tried to visit him once, but he preferred to see her at a later time. She understood he needed some time alone

Grieving is never easy... grieving with guilt is harder...

"Ariara! I was thinking... how about if we exchange some of these herbs with the nomads for new jars? These herbs can also be useful for them, no? Perhaps they can also help distribute these herbs to other villages. And you wouldn't have to spend so many coins anymore"

"Alright, smart boy. Do you know when the next tribe

will be coming by?"

He paused and did a mental count of days with his fingers, "Tomorrow... or the day after? Don't worry, you will be the first one I will tell of their arrival"

"I'm sure I will"

Aries placed several jars into his hand sack and left a few on the table for future bartering. They headed to the main village road. Aries joyfully handed jars to the villagers and happily collected their fruits and gifts in return whilst Ariara was caught up chatting with other folks along the way

Ariara noticed that Aries was giving extra jars to those bearing more gifts in return

"Help me understand. Why are you giving more jars to some people?"

"Ahh, that! I tried to decline receiving more gifts like you did in the past but they insisted. So I give them additional jar in gratitude"

"What about those who didn't give you any gifts in return?"

"As you said to give everyone who is in need, so I gave them too. Oh, and since I've collected more fruits - more than enough for you, Mandana, and myself - I also gave away some to those who didn't bring us any"

"Surely!" she raked his hair in approval

They moved towards the centre of the village. Ariara was on the lookout, hopeful to find Mandana but she was nowhere in sight. Aries was down to the last couple of jars. After he distributed them all, he bid her farewell

"See you tomorrow"

Back in her cave, a warm mid-afternoon breeze blew through. Laying down, resting, she admired Mandana's tapestry on the wall. Once, she had been so enamored by Dunya's etchings of the Golden light in the valley, hidden behind. But today, it was the beautiful tapestry itself which caught her attention… feather like forms, intricately circular… like a winged wheel…

The Wheel… of Life? That's what Mandana mentioned before! She never finished explaining it to me...

She took the short walk to Mandana's cave. When she

arrived, she called her name but there was no sign of her anywhere. She noticed Mandana's open journal on the floor by the entrance. Normally she wouldn't pry, but she saw her own name written and couldn't help herself...

Ariara has been struggling through these past months without telling anyone... I'm disappointed with myself for not...

But what can I tell her?

Is heartbreak truly because of love? Should a broken heart be embraced?

Elation - disappointment - frustration... the frail capacity of intimacy. No one is exempt from the pain of loss and the process of letting go...

If one must, shed tears, scream, mourn, lament... so be it

The world is abundant after all

Underneath it all, the desire to be supremely conscious to stay in the present and yielding to the radical truth of what is... makes a headway to breaking free

What a journey it has been

It was in the process of breaking free that I finally knew what Love is

Ariara tried to put the journal down, but continued to read...

Late at night you came calling out my name
haggard, wearied, unkempt

You've taken for granted those who were there for you
Why have you forsaken those who love you?
Why have you forsaken yourself?

Chasing a floating feather - The farther it floats, the more you kept holding tight

You broke her heart, You broke my heart

How could you?

In the years gone by, I've learned to let you go, but last night I breathed, rage almost consumed me

Why do I still long for your kiss, your touch
It's just a bait... to a life in a rut

I hate myself for letting you in last night
Feeling a flash of hope for us, I hate
My heart raced as our lips touched, I hate

My breasts pressed to your chest, I hate
Your mouth to my open lips, I hate
Mentioned her name as you kiss my neck, I hate
I hate to hate - but I hate it all

Stop asking me about her
If you need to know, find it out for yourself
How could you stab a broken heart?
Stop bothering me
Stop. Just Stop

Go chase your feathers
Stay away... from me

Apple trees were my witnesses, made me forget you

Apple trees reminded me how I am supposed to be loved

Apple trees were my witnesses...

One finally gave up on you, I say sorry for your loss
One is still chasing after her own desires without you

Should I say sorry for your loss again?
Is that something you will understand?

You tell me you're sorry
Well, I'm sorry too
Chase what you desire
So it will come to you
Stay away... from me
I am good without you...

Jahan...

Ariara dropped the book, shocked, and looked around to make sure nobody saw her reading it. *Jahan? She's writing about Uncle?*

Without much thought, her feet led her up to the hill, to the Oak tree. As she walked by the village road side, she was even more acutely aware of Mandana's apple trees than ever before

She got to the top of the hill, and there she found Mandana

- sitting relaxed, leaning on the tree, looking at the valley, deep in thought. She slowly approached her, not wanting to disturb her quiet moment...

"May I... join you?"

"Sure dear. Come. Sit anywhere you like"

She laid her body against the huge root of the tree, leaned with her eyes closed beside her, and let a comfortable silence surround them. After having read her journal, she sensed Mandana was in pain. She may not be able to give any answers, but she wanted to be there for her

It was quite a long while before Mandana changed her position, crossed her legs, still facing the valley and spoke

"He may not have realized I was falling for him when he gave me that glimpse of passion... I had to step back and give it some thought. It was tough. I was younger, but even then I knew he didn't have the full capacity to give what I was looking for... Years, I've spent convincing myself I made the right choice of not giving in to the temptation... because he was not mine to have... he was married to Mithraia, your Aunt, my friend... I stopped myself... but the more I declined... the further he got away... and he jumped right next to a chance with her..."

Tears flowed down her cheeks

Ariara was overwhelmed by Mandana's sudden confiding in her with such a revelation. *Does she know I read her journal?*

Mandana continued, "I tried to rebuild my sense of self... believed that I was alright... that I will be alright... and luckily, with divine grace, I began to appreciate life... myself... the idea of him in my life slowly faded away... Everytime I see him with her, it didn't... doesn't matter as much anymore"

She turned her gaze to the roadside

"So many times I've doubted myself, thought I wasn't good enough. These apple trees were my witnesses. Now they are standing tall, serving their purpose, as I should do mine"

Ariara pushed the anxiety of whether Mandana suspected her of prying aside. She was there simply to console her friend in time of need, no matter how it all came about, "Mandana... our village relies on you. You're always so strong and positive... in you we draw strength..."

"I loved him enough to give a way for him to ease his

burden... his confusion... hoping he could mend things with his wife whom he had committed to... but... he chose to follow his desires... it's fun chasing a feather up in the air... Tomorrow doesn't just 'take care of itself'! We also have to take care of tomorrow. Living in the moment is being present in the moment... and making decisions you feel are good for you. Chasing ungrounded dreams are illusions... I don't do well in that"

Ariara nodded in agreement

Mandana gazed at the valley as she softly spoke...

"Letting go of what no longer serves you is, to me, the ultimate sense of being free"

Ariara let some time pass before she spoke, "I was admiring your tapestry this morning, the wheel of life that you mentioned before. Could you please tell me more about it?"

"The wheel of life continually spins... It all seems so easy when we're on top... then... the consequences of our past actions and desires put us to the grind. We experience down lows, hopelessness... feels like it eats all of our energy, you and me know, as this Oak tree has witnessed"

"How can we avoid being carried away by the high ups and down lows?"

"Imagine a continually spinning wheel. Where do you think is the most grounded spot to be in?"

"Uhmm... in the middle? Since it stays where it is however the wheel turns"

"Exactly. But it is connected to the ends of the wheel... just like how in life we are all connected. Our decisions and actions will eventually impact those surrounding us. We also learn from the experiences of others, of those ahead of us, the wisdom of age, and even the innocence of youth. But our best bet would be to always move deeper, inside us, the most grounded place we can ever be, where the answer to our deepest question lies"

"And the feathers surrounding the wheel?"

"Ah, that was for Dunya... She's the feathery one..."

As Ariara was drifting off to sleep, she was enticed by a slight glimmer of the Golden Light. She closed her eyes tighter to ensure that she wouldn't lose it. This was the first time she had glimpsed it since her vision, and the first time it came to her room

Please, bring me back to him, bring me back to the desert...

The light broke into pieces - like a puzzle - and when it was put back together, she saw her uncle, weeping, alone...

Poor Uncle

He looked up as if he heard her voice, or up to the heavens, cursing the very sky for his misfortunes

She could see into his heart and feel his anguish

The day after - Ariara grabbed a pen and started to write...

seeker of freedom in misery

rest if you must
there is no need to rush
feel the air... breathe
let go of intolerable desires
feel the air... breathe
let go of fear
feel the air... breathe
let go of control
breathe...
let go of anything beyond bearing
you always got... you
walk your way back to you
your truth may be dimmed for now
with tempered vitality you'll know
in time

trust yourself

my oasis is my truth
on which I stand
on which I love

I raise my cares up high
I'm learning to let go when it's time to
peace of mind and heart, I seek
It's a new day to be present and live in the moment

She walked around her garden, feeling the fresh air. There was no intolerable pressure from outside of her. No thoughts boggled her mind. No more wonderment of, 'what could have been…'

When you let go of worries, you are free. All is well…

She heard wind whispers, birds chirping, as she walked amidst her creation, where each unique living thing, each stem gave pleasure and served a purpose in her life

A Soft, jolly voice from behind her said, "Here you are! I've been looking for you"

She continued her stroll, but replied in a friendly tone, "Good Morning Mandana. Such a lovely day today. How are you?"

Mandana kept pace with her, "A note from Dunya came in today"

She stopped and turned to face Mandana, "Oh?"

"Yes. A tribe arrived at dawn. When I went for my early walk, I saw Aries. He was heading to your cave but I told him to let you sleep in more. We went to meet them. The same tribe that Dunya went with and…"

Before she could continue, Aries' voice filled the air. He ran towards them and called their names in his musical way

Mandana winked at Ariara, "Buckle up dear! He's bringing you a big surprise"

"Dunya's cave is all cleaned up," Aries, out of breath from running, reported to Mandana

Ariara took one more sniff of her flowers before turning to greet Aries. She was, indeed, surprised to see a man following close behind him. The man lightly raked and tousled his own dark brown hair, radiating forth a happy spirit. His eyes, intense and gentle, met her gaze

A cold wind that had long been trapped in the chambers of her heart broke loose, as he introduced himself

"I'm Etoile"

"I'm... Ariara"

"The lady with herbs... pleasure to meet you, Ariara"

"Ah, yeah..." She nodded gently, smiled, lost for words

"I've heard so many great things about you from Dunya. I came here to personally thank you and Mandana for helping Wadjuri"

Mandana, thrilled to see Ariara's reaction, couldn't decide whether to leave her arms hanging at her sides or crossed over her chest. She whispered in Ariara's ear, "Twin brother... Just arrived today. Apparently, our Dunya asked him to look for me. We got him situated at her cave"

Aries was proud to show Ariara a sack of colored jars, "Look what he brought us!!"

Etoile looked into Ariara's eyes as he spoke, "Dunya said you might be able to use some of these"

"Hmm..."

"And I brought you some seeds I've collected from my travels, rare ones. They'll make beautiful additions to your garden"

As he handed her the packet of seeds and his hands touched hers, a sudden surge of emotion filled her. She stared at the pack, her mind slowly unraveling tangles of thoughts as she breathed deeply and looked straight into his eyes, with her genuine smile

Just like the Etoile I remembered...I'm so happy you found me... all is well...

The next day, Ariara leisurely strolled around the village, pleasantly greeting everyone she met. Their smiles, filled with gratitude and respect, warmed her heart

Such a beautiful day...

At the village centre, she found Mandana with a basket full of apples sitting amidst a small crowd laughing boisterously whilst she told a story. Mandana's words became clearer as she approached. Her voice and expression built suspense as she spoke

"... and when the king opened the door... Bam! He flew

into a rage!! There, in front of his very own eyes, in his very own bed, was his wife... and his most trusted guard. She hurried out of the room! His actions were swift and furious! In his hand, he held that famous note from the mystic...The dragon on the seal seemed to breathe fire as he rushed to the swordsmith's cave... he picked up a sword..."

Mandana noticed Ariara had joined the audience, "Good Morning dear. You missed out on my scary story"

"Scary?" Ariara scanned the crowd to see some of the listeners rolling on the ground, laughing

"The old story of the mystic's oracle... it is a scary one... I suppose..." She rolled her eyes and smiled in a cheeky manner

"Yeah, scary... and funny with your eyes rolling!" a lighthearted voice from the crowd followed by another loud laughter

"Mandana! Go on... what happened to his wife? The guard?" the crowd shouted excitedly

"No, no, no..." She teased, "That's the part of the story that's never to be mentioned ever again..."

As the crowd sighed in unison and slowly dispersed, Ariara saw that Etoile had been part of the audience. He noticed her and walked towards her, beaming

"Beautiful day"

"Oh hello. A beautiful morning indeed!"

Mandana joined them. Etoile teased her, "When will you reveal how the story ends?"

"We all know, it is what it is... end of story..." her voice had a vulnerable tone but her eyes expressed strength and gaiety, "However, it did give birth to all the apple trees we have by the roadside now"

Ariara laughed

Etoile was puzzled, "Apple trees?"

Aries jumped out from nowhere and raced beside Etoile, "I'm back, are you ready?"

"You shocked me boy! What are you up to now?" Mandana asked, whilst wiping away the feathers and leaves from Aries' clothes with care

"Etoile asked me to take him to the governor's cave"

"Uncle? Why?"

Etoile answered on his own behalf, "Dunya gave me a note for him, with strict instructions to deliver it personally. And... I too want to meet him. Perhaps there's something I can help with in the village, whilst I'm here"

Aries, seeming a bit worried that might lose his new found friend, tugged on Etoile's sleeve to get his attention, "You're not leaving soon, are you?"

Etoile patted him on the head lovingly, "Hmm... we'll see... that's why you need to introduce me to the governor so I'll have good reason to stay here"

"Oh, there's plenty to do around here. I'm sure he will have something for you to do!" Aries smiled and replied confidently, grasping Etoile's hand tightly

Etoile's gaze caught Ariara's. The light breeze glided through her and teased her hair as she flashed an affectionate, authentic smile and slowly turned towards the roadside

Aries pulled Etoile's arm, interrupting, "Come, let's go

this way. The Governor's cave is this way..."

Etoile bid farewell with fondness, before walking away with Aries

Ariara and Mandana headed towards the roadside. Mandana held an empty basket in one hand, and the other hand clasped around Ariara's arm. They walked leisurely, lighthearted and happy as apple-picking companions. Although they walked side by side, Ariara knew they were both in their own thoughts

Mandana spoke first, "Have you met up with your uncle? Since your aunt's passing?"

"Not yet. I visited him once, he suggested we meet another time"

"I'm glad that Aries and Etoile are paying him a visit. Perhaps that will help him get out of this dark place. I haven't seen him since..."

"Don't worry. Aries is good at making good things happen... he'll be able to arrange it"

"Arrange for Etoile to stay longer? He seems very eager to spend time with you... Isn't that sweet, dear?" Mandana brushed elbows with Ariara, teasing her

Ariara wiped an apple and took a bite, "Hmm... well... these apples are sweet.."

"Aren't you excited he's here?

"Of course I am! I was surprised when he first showed up in my garden. And I'm surely glad that he's here without... a beloved!

"Then why do I get the feeling that you're avoiding him? Are you, dear?"

Ariara paused for a while, took another bite of the apple, her whole body facing Mandana. She placed her hand on her chest, closed her eyes, felt the cool breeze, and took a deep breath. Then she opened her eyes, smiled in calm surrender and responded to her soul friend

"Avoiding? No. But I have no expectations. Those

moments of bliss that I had with him were in my vision... and they'll stay there. Unless it becomes manifested into my reality. Mandana, you're the one who told me, 'oases need to be sustainable.' We'll see what happens"

Mandana was tickled, "Oh well, c'mon now... smile a little.. laugh a little... you know... your authentic smile makes the world brighter... like a star..."

"I know," Ariara replied confidently with a sly smile and took another bite

They walked back home. Both enjoying the sight of Love Valley, and comforted by the sight of a certain, special Oak tree atop the hill. After all the turbulence and emotional storms had passed, they had found themselves walking with a familiar soul, with peace of mind and heart

Indeed, I'm a lucky star

In her cave, Ariara sat by her window admiring the calm of the valley. Over it, the moon she had danced, dreamed,

and explored with, eased its way slowly to eclipse the sun…
a celestial moment she had never witnessed before…

Strange emotions stirred within her. As the sun appeared to be consumed, unfamiliar fears emerged… *What is it? What am I fearful of? What am I afraid of losing? What am I afraid of letting go of? Why do I feel this way?*

Despite the eerie ambiance, the moon was a force, a magnet she couldn't resist. Without another minute wasted, she stepped out of her cave, barefoot, cinch pouch wrapped tightly around her left wrist

As she approached the valley, walking forward, onward, unrevealed fears slowly dissipated once the moon had fully covered the sun…

At her usual spot, she stood in calm surrender. The moon's force continued to draw her in, towards a new unknown. The feeling of absolutely new possibilities captured her imagination whilst a cool breeze drifted slowly by, ruffling her dress

To the moon… Her eyes wide open, the weight of her stare maintained, prolonged, visions flashed rapidly as she recited softly

moon's beautiful embrace, appease me
visions of the unknown, I see
I desire to go to the depths, the uncharted territories of my being,
the deepest recesses of my mind, my heart

transcendental warmth of the desert...
unrevealed longing, sparked...
by chance... I fell in love

what could have been, I no longer dwell, I was groggy...

drifted back to reality...

feeling deprived, I've been
inevitable grief, I endure
until all of me was spent
grasped for air, I breathe
in loneliness... solace, I find
by choice, I let go...

as seasons change, so did I

life goes on, so must I
past and present, life in cycles
karma I endured, lessons learnt
familiar souls realized, my soul tribe

what could have been, I no longer dwell
memories of heartbreak, I now cherish
kindness to others, forgiving
kindness to myself, healing

should I stay in love?
by efforts revealed, I'll discern

the beatific stars filled the sublime skies
the moon, exalted
it brings eternal promise
thou my purpose, just being, actualized
as long as I can breathe, freely
All is well

The last snippets of her vision were vivid, scattered, like lightning from a distant horizon

A charioteer flew his flying carriage over a well lit village where there was a great celebration... A sensational feast...

A glorious cup of love, overflowing, floated in the air...

A fiery wand with a blazing trail blasted through the sky... revered by everyone... leaves in the air like confetti....The celebratory feast continued...

A gigantic stone pentacle fell from the heavens. Its impact caused a massive shift of landforms like a volcanic eruption. Gold dust scattered in the new dawn. Total peace was felt in the village... in the valley...

Then, a sophic voice echoed in the wind... a mystic stood in the middle of the valley...

the road ahead, obscure as it should be...
be unburdened, you will uncover more...
experience it... live it...
life's magic continues...
Uphold your Truth

The ground trembled... gradually... a majestic sword, reverberating inevitable birth, a victory wreath hung over it, as it rose up to the sky. The new day begins...

Next day, The village was serene. The morning sun shone brightly over Ariara's garden. Morning dew dropped to the ground as she leisurely walked past her plants, hands extended. Each leaf swayed to the rhythm of her soft hum, welcoming her. Her plants opened up to a new day. The sun warmed the ground. Chirps of energetic little birds made a choral perimeter around her garden

Another beautiful morning...

"Beautiful morning, my lady"

That familiar voice. His words...

"Hey you!" She turned around to face him, took the time to look him in the eyes, appreciating his handsome features, "What brought you here this early?"

"I went for a quick stroll in the valley earlier... thought you might like these." He handed her a bunch of wild herbs and flowers. "I picked them on the way"

They continued to stroll side by side

Ariara blushed, "Much appreciated"

"I'm just warming up..." He moved closer to her side as they strolled, and continued in a gentle sensuous voice, "I want us to get to know each other better..."

"Hmm... let me think about that..."

"Why? Is there any reason why we can't?"

"I'm not sure... You're only going to be here for a short time?"

"That depends. If I stay, will you say yes?"

"Hmm... maybe..."

"Well, my tribe left last night... and I'm still here"

Surprised, she suddenly turned towards him, looked him straight in the eye, pursed her lips to hide her excitement, "Hmm... What made you stay?"

"Well, I didn't want to miss the chance to hand you flowers in the mornings"

"Haha... sweet talker are we? Ok, given that's true, alright... and?"

"Your uncle"

"You're staying for my uncle?"

"Your uncle told me how much you like wild flowers from the valley..."

She laughed, "Well, I'm glad you're staying. My plants would love to have you around to greet them in the mornings," she replied gleefully

"Just your plants?"

"Haha... the apple trees too!"

"What's the story behind these apple trees? You and Mandana seem to be sharing some great secret?"

"It's the secret that makes the apples so delicious, no?"

They continued to stroll, engaging in pleasant conversation. All at once, they heard a very loud commotion from a distance, villagers gathering, sounding like a flood about to rush into the village...

Aries voice trumpeted upon seeing Ariara and Etoile, "Wow!!! This is the biggest I've ever seen!" He stood in awe, whilst Etoile and Ariara joined him

The arriving tribe exuded a distinguished, flamboyant,

and vigorous aura. They possessed confident stances, moved unhurriedly as they unpacked trunk-loads of lavish merchandise

Out from one of the finely decorated carriages stepped a man slightly taller than Etoile. His clothes were dazzling. Confident and smart, he nonchalantly looked around, feeling the vibe of this new place. He inhaled. In a short meditative moment, his arms extended wide. He slowly blinked, as if absorbing the new energies into his body to ground him

With a nod, Etoile invited Ariara and Aries. They approached the carriage. The man's eyes sparkled with joy when he spotted Etoile

"My friend! I'm so pleased to see you!"

They shared a quick hug

"Welcome to our village!" Aries came in with the next hug. He took his time to admire, touch, the man's clothes, "Wow... you must have spent a lot of coins on these!"

Ariara took a closer look at the man's face, she stopped

He looks so familiar... Where have I seen him?

His eyes met hers. He looked surprised but kept his cool

"Ariara?" he whispered calmly

Ariara, grasping for words, smiled, squinted, "Hmm... yes I'm Ariara..." in hopes that the man would introduce himself

"I knew it! I'm Salem!"

"Salem?!"

She was flabbergasted, flushed...

I'll never forget you...

"How do you know each other?" Etoile asked, noticing his friend's magnetic pulse towards Ariara

Tongue-tied, she wondered how this strikingly appealing, grownup Salem could have wandered out of her visionary dream...

"From my dream..." Salem answered under his breath, enigmatically, so only she could hear, whilst holding his tantalizing gaze fixed on her. He touched her hair gently, rested his hand on her shoulder... savoring the moment

Etoile cleared his throat. Salem turned to him, wrapped his arm around his shoulder, "Glad we meet again, my friend"

"Are you gonna be staying for long?" Aries asked, hopeful for a yes. "I'll need lots of time to look through all these goodies you've brought in"

"Perhaps... especially now I have more reason to..." He tousled Aries' hair. Ariara couldn't help but notice Salem's childlike charm. She smiled pleasantly

"Yes!!" Aries jumped with joy

"Shall we go to my cave so you can get some rest after this long journey?" Etoile asked Salem. "I want to catch up with you, my friend!"

"Wow! You have a cave here? You move fast! Alright then, let's go! You need to tell me how I can get myself one too!"

Etoile winked at Ariara, "I'll see you later. I'm going to get him situated." He said as he softly waved goodbye

"Alright. Be well, both of you. Let us know if there's anything we can do to help." She turned to Aries. "Let's go to Mandana's. I'm sure she'll be interested to see all this new stuff here…"

As they walked back towards the village, Aries' excitement was still over the top. He kept looking back at the two men chatting, getting ready to go to Etoile's cave

Ariara was still feeling slightly shocked about Salem and his 'dream'

Did he have the same vision?

"There's no one here…" Aries observed, as they arrived at Mandana's empty cave

"She must have gone to check out the new arrivals"

"But she wasn't there either"

"Well, she must have walked by the other road, by the village roadside or the garden side. Who knows?"

"Ok, well, let's go do some work in the garden"

"Not now... I need to check on something else in my cave. Go enjoy the day"

Aries nodded, kicked a pebble, waved goodbye, and ran back towards the village centre. Before going home, he bumped into some kids by the well, decided to stay a while and play knucklebones with them

She sat by her window, folded left wrist beneath her chin. Still puzzled about how the morning had unfolded, she opened her pouch, took out the hourglass and placed it by the window. She watched the desert sand sifting down, down...

With the passage of time, the dust settles... Etoile is here to stay... and now the Best Camel Boy is also here as a dazzling man with dreams and visions... and eyes so scintillating, quite impossible to ignore

With her hand on her tummy, she whispered, *Stop... Butterflies... Stop...*

She couldn't help but laugh a little, as she made her way out for a walk to the valley, delighted

Ariara came knocking at Mandana's door the next day...

"Hello dear. Come on in. You're right on time. I'm making some final touches..."

Ariara's attention was immediately directed towards the beautiful artwork Mandana had in hand. It was a headdress of cascading feathers, reminiscent of the wheel of life tapestry she had woven for Dunya, long ago

Ariara gasped, "It's Beautiful..."

"Well, rightfully so, as it is for a beautiful soul... and a dear friend."

Mandana placed the headdress on Ariara's head. She cupped her face with both hands, and gave her a quick kiss on her forehead

"Oh! For me? You make me feel like a queen!"

It fits perfectly. Mandana stroked her hair so that the trailing ends merged seamlessly

"Lovely! You look lovely dear," she was elated to see Ariara so charmed

"Thank you Mandana! I love it! Let's see, you wove a tapestry for Dunya... and a headdress for me? Do I really need that much of a reminder to ground myself? That I need to wear it on my head?"

Mandana giggled and looked afar, as if recollecting a distant memory, "It's kind of a secret reminder since you don't see it right away... But this one here, on your head, let it remind you that every time you want to follow your heart, don't forget what your head says too... They must align... Love, with all its intricate twists and turns, need not be avoided. After all, Love is the most beautiful feeling on earth... it allows us to grow. Let this be a reminder to strive to be the epitome of balance and gracefulness, even in love"

"Thank you Mandana... honestly, I'm not sure if I could ever have made it this far without you..."

"Of course you could have! No doubt about that. All this while... you always have you... you learned and you're strong. I was here just to chat about tree planting!"

"I mean, I never knew about the oasis..."

"You would have figured it out in time dear. We all do. That powerful source from within, that magical wind that carries us through life, and your discernment got you here"

"Thank you... I appreciate having you in my life so much, Mandana." She hugged her tight, "Oh, by the way, we couldn't find you yesterday"

"Oh, I just needed some time alone to think"

"You missed out on the arrival of Etoile's friend...the new tribe... Salem, the Camel Boy..."

"Salem the Camel boy? Do I know him? The name sounds familiar..."

Ariara laughed, "Remember from my desert vision? The Camel Boy I was telling you about..."

"Desert vision? Ahhh, the Camel boy! What do you

mean? He's here?"

"Yes! It seems he decided to grow up and meet me here. Mandana, I think he also had visions of meeting me... but we didn't get a chance to speak much about the details"

Suddenly, Aries barged in - excited as usual

"Salem is staying! And..." he stopped for a moment, raising the anticipation of the two women, eyes wide as he continued, "The governor agreed to have a feast tonight for all of the village. Everyone is invited!"

"A feast?"

"Yeah! Salem wants to get everyone together so he could meet them all. He's going to be staying here for a while"

"Hmm... Seems this 'camel boy' knows exactly how to make a grand entrance!" Mandana teased, bumping elbows with her

Aries could barely contain his excitement, "Salem said he will give me something nice to wear! I'm going to his carriage now to choose... Wait... why did you call him 'this Camel Boy?'"

Mandana laughed. Ariara blushed

Aries rustled his own hair as he walked away. He didn't understand what the ladies were laughing about, but was too excited to ask any further questions

Ariara unconsciously touched her new headdress and gracefully moved her neck side to side, admiring how beautifully the feathers flowed over her hair

"Oh! I hope you'll wear that to the feast!" Mandana said lovingly

"Of course I'm going to! You know, by the way, I came here to tell you about another vision I had that night when the moon eclipsed the sun... I saw a charioteer with a magnificent chariot flying into the village, much like how Salem's grand entrance was like today... and there was a feast too..."

"You saw this one coming dear?"

"Yes, I must have"

"What else did you see?"

"A cup overflowing with love... a fiery wand blasted

through the sky, a gigantic stone pentacle fell from the heavens... then there was total silence... and the mystic... the dragon coin mystic appeared and spoke... 'Experience it... Live it... Life's magic continues...'

"Wow! Her message was so simple yet so powerful... Life's magic continues. Indeed, yes, and it's another new day"

"Exactly!"

It was mid-afternoon when Salem directed the members of his tribe to pack up their merchandise and start setting up for the night's feast

They all helped in the transformation of the village centre. The women raised tents around the perimeter. Along with colorful woven blankets and ground pillows, they scattered multicolor mosaic covered lamps along the grounds

Some of the men set up and tuned musical instruments in one corner. Assorted drums, chimes and horns lined a long table. More tables and benches were placed at various angles, making it so that everyone could enjoy the food and music together

Salem walked to and fro, making sure everything was perfect. He glowed in the warm ambiance brought by the lamp lighting. He told one of his men to start a centre bonfire at night fall, and a few more bonfires around the centre. He wanted it to be just perfectly bright with warmth. When some men started to bring in cooked meat, grains, fruits and drinks to the centre, he went back to his carriage to get dressed

The villagers strolled in. Children played, jumping around and tumbling on the colorful pillows strewn about. Women came prepared with pleasantries in long and short dresses, handmade necklaces and colorful hair ties

The governor arrived with his men carrying even more food and drink. One of Salem's men approached the governor and led him to the centre table, seated him in the middle as per Salem's instruction. The musicians played. Immersed in the vivacious festivity, he was amazed at how the village had been transformed so merrily in such a short time

Mandana wore a nicely fit dress flowing just a little below her knees, in vivid colors. The festive aura of the village centre at once made her elated. Ariara wore a shorter dress, flowing above her knees, in pale neutral color. The feathers on her headdress were the primary accents of her clean, mystical ensemble. Her cinch pouch on her wrist as always. They sat at the Governor's table

Next to arrive was Aries, excited as usual. His parents settled in one of the tents and mingled with the tribes. He, on the other hand, sat right next to the governor as if he was an invited dignitary

"I brought flowers from our garden"

"Ah! So nice of you! You're looking quite handsome, young man"

"Salem got me these!" He stood up straight and proud. Showing off the fine fabrics and exquisite tailoring

"Wow, you got a new friend I see. You look grand. And those flowers look so healthy. Your time spent helping Ariara in her garden is really paying off well"

"Yes, she's teaching me so much! I know the names of all the herbs and what they are helpful for. Oh, and we're planning to provide for nearby villages too. Have you seen the jars we have in the garden, those colored ones? I selected those"

"Hmm, yes, I have noticed those. Most importantly, thank you for watching over Ariara. She's very precious to me. I don't want her to be in any danger whatsoever"

The governor winked at Ariara and Mandana as he patted Aries on the head

Aries replied casually as he eyed the tremendous spread of food with awe, "There's so much food!"

"Of course! It's a feast!" Salem's voice bellowed from behind as he joined them

"Woow!" Aries was out of words, as his attention shifted from the food to Salem's glimmering attire

He was dressed in an elegantly sewn tunic and trousers, nicely fit with more vivid colors than anyone had ever seen. He approached the governor with a friendly vibe and firm handshake

"Mandana whispered to Ariara, "This is the '*Camel boy*'? That's no boy for sure! That man is one beautiful piece of art!"

The Governor stood to greet him, "Here you are. This

handsome young man was just telling me you gave him his magnificent clothes tonight"

Aries smiled proudly

Salem gave Aries a playful jab as he walked past him to the other side of the table, "This handsome young man has been great company since I got here. Never let me out of his sight"

Aries spoke with full confidence, "Of course! I'm expecting your help with our new plan to distribute herbs to the nearby villages... Ariara and I are planning this..."

"You and Ariara have plans?" Salem asked with a funny tone and winked at Ariara

"Uh-huh, we have not fully discussed it yet but we will..."

The governor laughed, "Sincerely, Salem, thank you for this feast," he surveyed the festival, "All of the villagers are merry and lively!"

Salem, very well mannered, bowed to the Governor and sat next to Ariara

She blushed as he took her hand in his for a greeting

He spoke softly, "You are as beautiful as I remember, my desert flower"

"Desert flower? I didn't know I was given that name..."

"In my dream," he glanced up to the skies, then to her and smiled

"Hmm.. was it in *your* dream or... mine?" Ariara asked, her smile demure

"Does it matter?" Short and composed, he replied, profoundly relishing this whimsical rendezvous as the rest of the table chatted

"As I recall... you could barely speak to me then..." Ariara said coyly, recalling his pure spontaneous gesture when giving her the hourglass

"Perhaps, it wasn't the right time to speak"

"Perhaps? hmm..."

"It's about time we meet again. It's quite amazing, no?

You were wearing this lovely tunic, just like tonight..." His tantalizing gaze swooped from her eyes to her lips, then shifted away in composed countenance

"And what about the camels?"

"Camels?"

"Never mind..."

"I didn't come here to disappoint you, desert flower. If you like camels, I can arrange for camels to be brought here"

"Ah... no thank you. I was just curious about your dream... plus it will take some time to get them into the village!"

"In my dream I saw how much you enjoyed being at a feast. So I made sure this happened on my arrival"

"A feast, huh? And you're making it happen exactly as in your vision?" *He's got a different vision... his own vision...*

"I knew there would come a time that I'd see you in reality. Now is that moment," he softly whispered in her ear

Mandana, cleared her throat as if she was about to say something but was interrupted by Etoile's arrival at the table. Salem was the first to greet him. After greeting everyone at the table, he sat next to Ariara. She was still blushing from her dreamy talk with Salem

"Did I miss something?" Etoile asked, boyishly

Ariara didn't know how to answer, but she was saved by the governor raising his voice to get everyone's attention

"Salem. Etoile. I want to welcome you both to our village. It's an honor to have you here. You are welcome to stay as long as you like. Now, let's eat this delicious food..."

Mandana cleared her throat again. "I'd like to say something first. Salem, thank you for doing this for us! It's such a lively, beautiful feast... and it's quite fortunate for me to have you all here because I have an announcement to make... since we are together on this beautiful night, celebrating each other's presence, life... Well, I've been thinking for a while..."

"This suspense is killing me, what is it?" The governor asked impatiently

"Calm down, relax, ease up, Jahan, I'll get to my point, alright" She paused, had a sip of her drink

"I've decided to travel, step out of the village for a while... see new places, new scenery, make new acquaintances..."

"Travel? Alone? Why would you do that?" Jahan asked

"Because I want to, and I'm excited about it"

Ariara looked at her soul friend and saw how delighted Mandana was. She was beaming, seemingly from this new desire to embark on a journey... *to find her own oasis*

"I'm happy that you're doing this for yourself Mandana," Ariara hugged her tight, trying to hide her teary eyes

Mandana comforted her, "I just need you to watch over my trees whilst I'm gone"

"Of course I will. Your trees and I will be here when you are ready to find your way home"

"Something we can cheer about tonight, yes? Let's raise our drinks for Mandana!" Salem stood and raised his cup

Everyone followed suit. Jahan, reluctantly, did as well, "I'm not sure... if... that's really a good idea... the village without you here will..." He stammered

"Jahan, dear, I'm not gonna disappear like..." She tactfully stopped herself from opening old wounds, "I'm simply going to travel and when I'm done with what I need to do, to see... I'll find my way home"

Ariara added, "We will be alright. Once Mandana has fulfilled what she needs to do, she'll find her way back home, Uncle. That's all we need to know"

Suddenly, Ariara saw a glimpse of her vision... when the fiery wand blasted through the skies... then she looked at Mandana, laughing, genuinely happy... *the fiery wand was Mandana's fire...*

"Mandana, how will you leave the village? You will need a carriage? Salem has a lot, but..." Aries innocently asked, thinking about the logistics

"Aries! You never fail to plan, boy, I'll figure that out"

Salem openly suggested, "Well... Since I'll be here for a while, let's go with Aries' plan. You can take one of my carriages. One of my men can drive for you, and I'll send a maiden along to assist you... what do you say?"

"That's more than what I would have expected, and yes, I'll take it! Thank you for your kindness Salem. You are a blessing from the skies. Thank you!" Mandana replied and gazed at Ariara as if mentally conversing with her to remember how this charioteer came into the village as per her vision

Ariara winked back and leaned in towards Salem, "Thank you Salem, it means a lot. I want Mandana to be safe in her travels"

Mandana blushed, "Thank you dear. Now enough about me, shall we continue with our festivities? Salem what else do we have in line for tonight?"

"Dancing!" Salem shouted with excitement, as he waved at the band to play a lively song. Then he turned to Ariara and extended his hand for a dance. Simultaneously, Etoile did the same

Ariara froze for a bit, didn't know what to say. Another glimpse of her vision flashed in her mind... the gigantic stone pentacle falling from the heavens, gold dust scattered all around...

"The world is abundant... opportunities are everywhere... and we have the whole night to dance, gentlemen... take turns..." Mandana came to the rescue and smiled knowingly to Ariara before turning to Jahan, "Come, let's dance, for old times... I'll tell you more about my travel plans. And... it's about time we talk"

She stood up and fixed her dress. Jahan stood, followed Mandana to the centre where some villagers had already started to dance

"Who will dance with Ariara first?" Aries asked, looking at the two men with arms extended to Ariara. He flipped his coin...

Time stood still for Ariara... she felt a strong sense of peace... grounding... intention manifested in reality... sustainability... *exactly what I need in my oasis... the giant pentacle falling from the heavens was for me... I'll wait till the gold dust settles... no need to rush...*

"You go first. Dance. I'll take the next song. Aries and I have something important to discuss" Etoile acquiesced to Salem

Ariara accepted Salem's hand. She rose gracefully and

followed him to the centre. Looking back at Etoile, his gentle gaze on her, she gave him a genuine smile

They danced

"Do you mind if I put my arm behind your back, Ariara?" Salem asked as he reached for her back, drawing her closer

"Not at all... I'm sure you will not do anything to displease me"

"It's destiny that brought me here... to you. It may seem a little crowded now..." he glanced at Etoile briefly, "He's a very good friend of mine. But I'll take my chances"

Ariara smiled softly, remembering the boy she met in her vision of the desert

"I'll find my way there... my desert flower," Salem gestured towards her heart

"Hmm... what if it will take some time before... before we know what's destined?" Ariara replied

Salem paused and glanced up to the skies. When Ariara looked up she was sure that she caught a glimpse of golden dust softly sifting through an hourglass. She turned her attention back to a smiling Salem. He had a twinkle in his eye as he said, "I'll take the time"

The song ended. They went back to the table. Mandana and Jahan were eating. Aries was engaged in discussion with Etoile

Aries' excitement was overpowering, "Ariara, Etoile gave me some ideas on our herb distribution. You're going to love what we came up with..."

"Alright, alright! We will look into that tomorrow, Aries. Let's enjoy tonight first okay?"

"Okay!"

Salem moved on to mingling with his tribe and the rest of the villagers. They danced in a group. Food, fun and lively songs filled the rest of the evening

As the evening deepened, Jahan gave a short speech welcoming Salem as a new assistant officer in planning for improvements in the village, and expressing gratitude to him for arranging this feast that everyone so enjoyed. He also announced that Etoile, too, would be joining in the design and construction of new projects in the village. Everyone clapped and shouted joyfully in excitement

When it was time to call it a night, Ariara noticed Etoile approach Salem. They spoke briefly. She was unable to hear anything but their parting words for one another

"Well..." Etoile extended his hand for a firm handshake and continued, "Since you were fortunate enough to be Ariara's first dance, I'll walk her home tonight"

Salem nodded and tapped his friend's shoulder in agreement

Ariara bid goodbye to her uncle and hugged Mandana before turning to Etoile

"That looks good on you," Etoile lightly touched Ariara's headdress as he shyly began to start a conversation

"Thank you! Mandana made this for me"

"Did you enjoy the night?"

"Of course!"

"Salem is good at arranging such gatherings, making everyone feel good. I admire that in him"

Ariara smiled and nodded demurely in agreement. Etoile paused for a while, listening to the comfortable silence between them before continuing, "I'm happy for Mandana, that she has decided to travel. I have done much travelling myself..."

"Yes. My uncle's reaction earlier was quite uncalled for. But you know, they've known each other for the longest time... This is a big change for Mandana... and for him too..."

"I understand..."

"Seems like she's closing this chapter and heading for a brand new start"

"Ariara..." He stopped walking and faced her

"Yeah..." Ariara looked at him. Under the clear sky of night, his handsome features were undeniably irresistible

He briefly looked up and gazed back at her, reached for her hand and whispered, "For a brand new start..."

She smiled, "May I see your left palm?"

He drew closer to her and opened his left palm. She traced his palm lines forming a perfect...

He whispered again, "My Lucky Star"

She looked up to meet his gaze, a snippet of her latest vision flashed... once more, the giant pentacle from the heavens has finally landed on the ground, the earth palpitating like a heart... Golden dust scattered in the air

She blinked several times... looking for continuation of her vision, but all she could see in that moment was his charming face gazing at her... only at her...

"Your... Lucky Star?" She couldn't believe that she heard him right

"Yes, you are," He replied

His gaze was tender, drawing her in. He touched her cheek, her heart pumping as his lips softly brushed hers...

The next day she woke up early and sat by her window gazing out towards the Love Valley. It was still dark. With the first light of dawn, a snippet of her latest vision flashed to

mind... a majestic sword with a victory wreath hung over it rose up to the sky

Gradually, the panoramic view of the Love Valley was revealed... its serenity, so inviting... the new day begins...

She put on her headdress, grabbed her cinch pouch, and decided to take a walk towards the Love Valley. On the way, she spotted the hill and decided, instead, to visit her Oak tree

She sat under the Oak tree, cross legged, relaxed. She closed her eyes, breathed in... breathed out... listened to the wind... to all the early sounds of the morning

She opened her eyes and, as she was inclined to, her pouch, laying all she had on the ground... the stones from the mounds... the dragon coin... the feather... the hourglass... the star... the oak twig... the acorn...

She then turned her gaze at the uninterrupted view of the Love Valley...

My road to finding love was filled with fun, excitement, surprise... even tears and heartbreak. But the most essential part was knowing I need to know the Oasis I can thrive on... It was then that I found myself...

As the morning breeze drifted, cascading feathers from her headdress gently touched her face. She laid her palms on her head as she breathed in... and out... *The Wheel of Life on my head...*

Then she placed her right hand on her chest, over her heart... *with all the intricate twists and turns, balance and grace bring my heart and mind in alignment... I'll never shy away from Love... the most beautiful feeling on earth*

Printed in Great Britain
by Amazon

74266395R00095